american imperialism & anti-imperialism

D1298788

HURRAH FOR IMPERIALISM!

american imperialism & anti-imperialism

EDITED BY THOMAS G. PATERSON

University of Connecticut

problem studies in american history

Thomas Y. Crowell Company
New York
Established 1834

Library of Congress Cataloging in Publication Data

PATERSON, THOMAS G., ed.
  American imperialism and anti-imperialism.

  Bibliography: p. 141
    1. United States—Foreign relations—1897–1901
—Addresses, essays, lectures.   2. United States—
Foreign relations—1865–1898—Addresses, essays, lectures.
3. United States—Foreign relations—War of 1898—
Addresses, essays, lectures.   I. Title.
E713.P3   327.73   72–10238
ISBN   0-690-07130-2

FOR MY MOTHER AND FATHER,

SUZANNE AND THOMAS

PATERSON

The frontispiece is the cover illustration from Life, *16 June 1898.*

1   2   3   4   5   6   7   8   9   10

preface

In recent years, perhaps as never before, Americans have
been searching for the roots of their current foreign policy.
Those people eager for information to explain how the
United States became an interventionist global power have
found important continuities between the past and the
present. In the study of history they have discovered a
complex, tortuous, and decades-long story of American
ventures abroad. This book presents a significant part of that
history—the period of vigorous American expansion and
empire-building in the late nineteenth century.

I designed this book as a compact volume with the
necessary intellectual tools to interpret American
imperialism and anti-imperialism. Thirteen respected,
well-written, scholarly, and provocative essays from the
pens of distinguished historians tackle the general
questions suggested in the introduction. To add further
cohesion to this collection, I have included maps, a
chronological chart, brief headnotes, and an extensive
bibliography. The complexity of this historical topic,
however, is not sacrificed to misrepresentative simplicity.

For various suggestions, criticisms, and assistance I thank
Kenneth Culver, Kenneth Hagan, A. William Hoglund,
James Mylott, Janet Payne, Geoffrey Smith, and Arnold
Taylor. The cooperation of the authors and publishers of
the essays printed herein was appreciated. The dedication
hardly expresses the profound feeling a son has for his
parents, but does identify two very special people.

Thomas G. Paterson

chronology

1893

January: Hawaiian revolution; American marines from
  U.S.S. *Boston* helped dethrone queen
March: Cleveland withdrew treaty

1894

July: Wilson-Gorman tariff hurt Cuban sugar exports
  (to U.S.) and the Cuban economy

1895

February: Opening of Cuban revolution
July: Olney note to Britain on Venezuela

1896

February: General Weyler established "reconcentration"
  camps in Cuba
May: Spain rejected U.S. offer to help end Cuban war
August: Beginning of insurrection in Philippines
November: McKinley elected

1897

June: McKinley sent new Hawaiian treaty of annexation to
  Senate
November: Spain recalled Weyler, and reformed reconcentration policy

1898

February: deLôme letter and sinking of the *Maine* (Havana)
March: Congress appropriated $50 million for defense;
  Senator Proctor spoke on trip to Cuba
April: Spain accepted temporary armistice and revocation
  of reconcentration; McKinley asked Congress for war;
  Congress declared Cuba independent; Teller Amendment
  (U.S. not to annex Cuba);
May: Dewey defeated Spanish at Manila, Philippines
June: U.S. troops departed for Cuba; Guam seized
July: Battle of San Juan Hill; Wake Island seized;
  Hawaii annexed; Puerto Rico invaded; Spain asked
  for terms of peace
August: Hostilities suspended; U.S. captured Manila
October: American Peace Commission established
November: U.S. demanded Philippines; Anti-Imperialist League organized
December: Treaty of Paris

1899

February: Filipino armed revolt against U.S.; Treaty of
  Paris ratified by Senate;
September: Open Door notes

contents

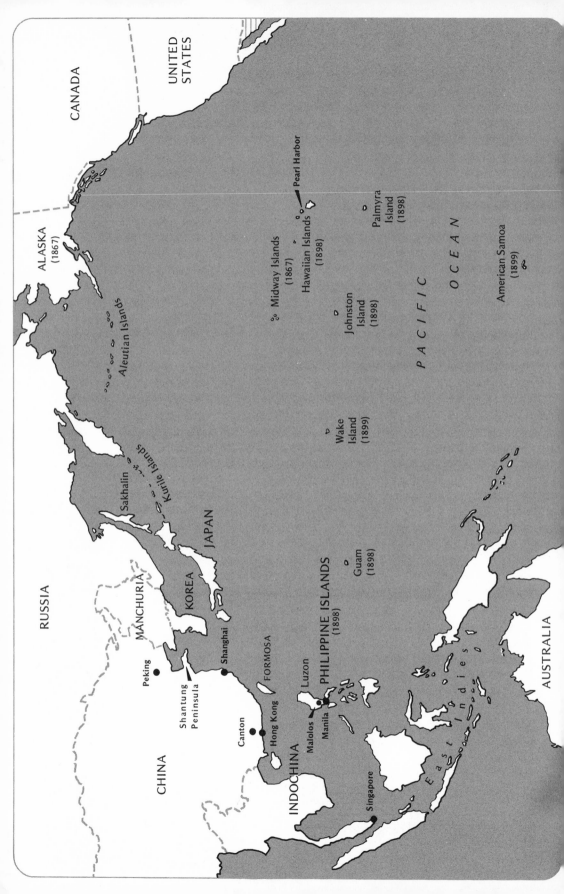

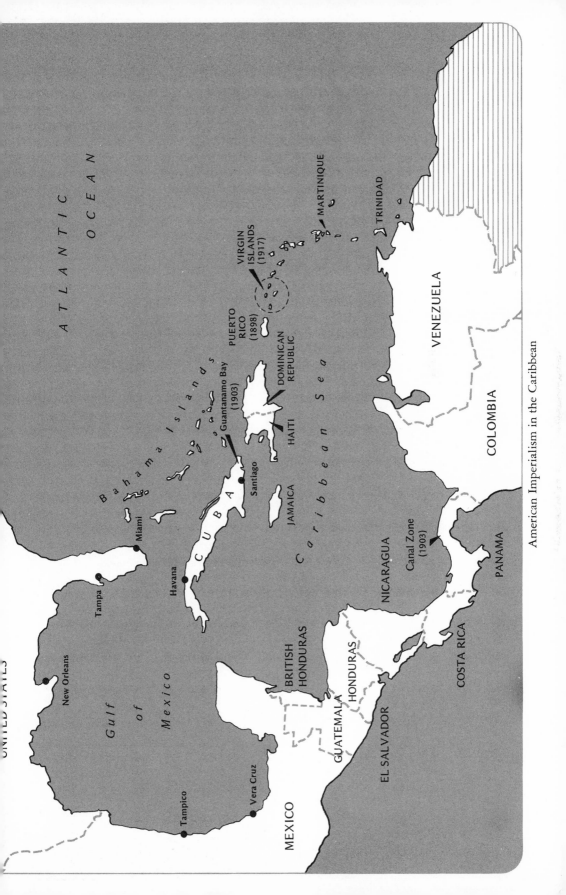

American Imperialism in the Caribbean

UNITED STATES

New Orleans

Tampa

Miami

Gulf of Mexico

Tampico

Vera Cruz

MEXICO

GUATEMALA

BRITISH HONDURAS

HONDURAS

EL SALVADOR

NICARAGUA

COSTA RICA

Canal Zone (1903)

PANAMA

ATLANTIC OCEAN

Bahama Islands

Havana

CUBA

Santiago

Guantanamo Bay (1903)

JAMAICA

Caribbean Sea

HAITI

DOMINICAN REPUBLIC

PUERTO RICO (1898)

VIRGIN ISLANDS (1917)

MARTINIQUE

TRINIDAD

COLOMBIA

VENEZUELA

introduction

After joining the European powers in competition for
colonies in the late nineteenth century, the United States
entered the twentieth century as the overlord of societies in
the Far East and Latin America. Much of the American
empire was formed in a burst of imperialist activity during
the late 1890s and early 1900s. But that imperialist
thrust met considerable opposition from anti-imperialists
in America and from nationalists in areas dominated by
Americans. Senator Henry Cabot Lodge, an articulate
imperialist, commented shortly after the Senate ratified the
treaty annexing the Philippines, Guam, and Puerto Rico
in February 1899 that the treaty passed only after the
"closest, most bitter, and most exciting struggle I have ever
known, or ever expect to see in the Senate." And the
126,000 American soldiers who battled thousands of
Filipinos until mid-1902 to subdue the new and rebellious
colony witnessed and practiced cruelties matched only by
the wars against American Indians. Contemporaries and most
scholars agree that the American foreign policy of the
late 1890s bequeathed to the twentieth century a deep and
durable record as well as a host of problems.

Although American imperialism appears minimal
compared to that of the European states, it is a major
question in American history and in the history of the
peoples Americans subjugated. The selections in this volume
will reveal how the empire-building of the 1890s divided
the American people, left scars at home and abroad,
questioned the nation's past and future, exposed the often
tangled roots of American principles and actions, and,
according to your persuasion, constituted either a noteworthy
aberration or a dramatic example of an expansionist
continuity in American foreign policy.

There are, of course, varying interpretations of American
imperialism. That variety is derived in part from the
differing definitions of the term and its casual use in
political campaigns and international ideological contests.
Some observers equate "expansion" with imperialism,
but others define imperialism as solely the annexation of
colonies or territory. Still other scholars define the term
more generally to mean the determining influence or control
over another people or region. The American domination
of Cuba for several decades after 1900 is by the first
and third definitions imperialism, but is not so by the

1

second. The acquisition of the Philippines is clearly imperialism by all definitions. One cannot attempt an interpretation of American imperialism until he has delineated lucidly his own definition.

Most definitions assume that superior power exists in the imperial nation and that that power is exerted against a weaker entity. Such power can be applied directly or indirectly, formally (institutionally) or informally, or through political, military, or economic means. Power is central, then. Yet historians differ widely in their explanations of why and by whom American imperial power was unleashed. The interpretive problem breaks down into at least three fundamental questions, to which the selections in Part I address themselves.

The first problem is one of political process. Was American power directed toward imperialist ventures by an elite holding decision-making authority, or by an influential pressure group, both of whom shaped public opinion? Or was it directed by an aroused popular will, by a mass movement of the American people that compelled reluctant leaders toward empire?

The second question centers on the rationality and consciousness of American imperialism. Was the exertion of American power for imperial purposes rational, deliberate, planned, and derived from a careful assessment of the American national interest? Or was it irrational, emotional, unintentioned, ill-planned, and derived from an ill-considered spur-of-the-moment response to explosive events and popular ideas?

The third question is that of motivation. Which motives best explain the American drive for empire: nationalism, with its components of pride, duty, racial superiority, and prestige; humanitarianism; economic necessity and ambition; domestic unrest; Social Darwinism; the restlessness of an adventuresome generation that had not participated in a war; international competition; or the perceived need for naval and strategic stations? If, as observers agree, a number of these motives were at work simultaneously, which motives, or combination of motives, were most significant?

There are some corollary questions that scholars usually address less directly or consciously but which are evident in the selections. Was the motivation for going to war with Spain the same as the motivation for annexing foreign real estate? Could the war have been avoided? Was the acquisition of the Philippines the only course available to the United States after Spain's defeat? And most scholars answer a moral question: Was American imperialism right (good) or wrong (bad)? Although in a more sophisticated way, historians tend to agree with either Emilio Aguinaldo, leader of the Filipino independence movement, that Americans were "the true oppressors of nations and the tormentors of mankind . . . ," or with President William McKinley, who prophesied that the Filipinos would "bless the American republic because it emancipated their fatherland, and set them in the pathway of the world's best civilization."

Water LaFeber, in *The New Empire: An Interpretation of American Expansion, 1860–1898* (1963), introduces these questions for this collection. He argues that elite businessmen, government officials, and popularizers (like Alfred T. Mahan) formulated an American imperialist position deliberately and rationally, based upon their concern for foreign markets. Like R. W. Van Alstyne (*The Rising American Empire* [1960]), LaFeber places the imperialism of the 1890s in the continuity of American expansion before the Civil War. LaFeber concludes, however, that a new type of American empire emerges after that conflict—an empire whose objective was markets rather than land. For LaFeber, Secretary of State William Seward (1861–69) was a significant and foresighted spokesman for the new economic empire but was stymied in his own day by anti-imperialists. What changes occurred in the United States after the 1860s to permit Seward's ideas to become influential later?

In 1895 Secretary of State Richard Olney lectured the British government that "To-day the United States is practically sovereign on this continent, and its fiat is law upon the subjects to which it confines its interposition." And Peter Finley Dunne satirized feverish nationalists through his Irish-American characters: 'We're a gr-reat people,' said Mr. Hennessy, earnestly.

'We ar-re,' said Mr. Dooley. 'We ar-re that. An' th' best iv it is, we know we ar-re.' From Seward's days to the early 1890s, the United States increased its influence in Hawaii, Samoa, and Cuba, and Latin America in general, declared the Monroe Doctrine to be an important international principle restricting European involvement in hemispheric affairs, expanded its trade, sought the principle of equal trade opportunity ("open door"), and through new construction and treaty ports improved considerably the fighting ability of its battle fleet. Many historians have depicted the Spanish-American War and the resultant territorial prizes as the culmination of America's evolving post-Civil War assertiveness and expansion.

William E. Leuchtenburg in his selection treats the war as an expression of popular American hunger for foreign ventures built up over a period of years. Tending to agree with George F. Kennan (*American Diplomacy, 1900–1950* [1951]) and Charles E. Osgood (*Ideals and Self-Interest in America's Foreign Relations* [1953]), who stress the mindlessness of the Spanish-American War, Leuchtenburg recounts a story of feverish public opinion, inflamed by unscrupulous journalism and conspicuous episodes like the sinking of the *Maine*. Aggressive public pressure forced a reluctant but weak president to war. In Leuchtenburg's judgment, it was a needless war, stumbled into without a thoughtful assessment of the American national interest and the consequences of empire. The American people got the war they wanted. Did they also get the empire they wanted?

Unlike LaFeber, Leuchtenburg largely ignores an explanation for the popular "taste of Empire." Granted that the noisy newspapers exaggerated events and aroused war fevers, why were Americans so eager for foreign venture and so receptive to journalistic propaganda? Richard Hofstadter suggests in his selection that the United States in the 1890s experienced a psychic crisis. That is, internal frustrations growing out of economic depression and domestic social disorders created an irrational penchant for aggression. Yet why did the McKinley administration respond to frustrations particularly by declaring war against a weak Spain and by annexing distant territories, instead of venting the frustrations in some other way?

Hofstadter recognized that his thesis did not consider how the political process functioned under the aura of the psychic crisis. Howard K. Beale discusses the question directly in the essay from his *Theodore Roosevelt and the*

Rise of America to World Power (1956). Beale is unequivocal in arguing that an alert coterie of imperialists clustered around Theodore Roosevelt planned American imperialism. Denying that mindless public opinion propelled America abroad, Beale believes that an imperialist clique, motivated by nationalism and racism, shaped public opinion. Does the historical record indicate a conspiracy? Roosevelt said that McKinley had "no more backbone than a chocolate eclair." Was a pusillanimous McKinley manipulated, as Leuchtenburg concludes, by public opinion, which was in turn shaped by Roosevelt, as Beale contends? Did the decision for war and empire rest with the president or with a group of plotters?

John A. S. Grenville and George B. Young dissent vigorously from Beale's interpretation of presidential weakness and imperialism by clique. Resurrecting McKinley's image, they join H. Wayne Morgan (*William McKinley and His America* [1963]) and Margaret Leech (*In the Days of McKinley* [1959]) in casting the president as a strong, courageous, and self-reliant leader who tried to keep the nation from war through careful diplomacy. Grenville and Young write that McKinley labored to cool a militant Congress and to follow a cautious diplomacy to gain Spanish concessions in Cuba, as well as Cuban acceptance of moderation in the revolution. Why have historians and Americans believed for so long that McKinley was a feeble leader? Do McKinley's actions demonstrate that he was a man of peace? Did he act in the national interest or in response to political pressure? Does the evidence suggest that the ultimate decision for war was made in Washington, in Madrid, or in Havana? Grenville and Young assume that McKinley had a right to demand that Spain solve the chaos in Cuba. It is an assumption that Morgan (*America's Road to Empire* [1965]) accepts but which other scholars question, because it presupposes that one nation has the right to impose its definitions of right on another, and that one nation can judge another and threaten intervention to bring about a desired result. In any case, Grenville and Young, as do others, insist that we assess McKinley's leadership.

Historians have long studied the role of American businessmen in the formulation of national policies. What role did businessmen play in American imperialism? And what was their relationship with McKinley? Until Julius W. Pratt published his *Expansionists of 1898* in 1936, it was commonly accepted that American business had been assertively expansionist and a major lobbying force behind McKinley's foreign policy. Pratt challenged that assumption and argued that businessmen were hesitant about pursuing action that might lead to war against Spain and that businessmen "had been either opposed or indifferent to the expansionist philosophy which had arisen since 1890." But why did businessmen change their minds about empire after war broke out? Is Pratt convincing about such a sudden reversal? For Pratt, business pressure and economic factors do not explain the Spanish-American War or American imperialism. Joining Leuchtenburg and Hofstadter, Pratt blames public opinion—but opinion stimulated by the idea of manifest destiny, missionary zeal, and Social Darwinism. A number of historians, especially LaFeber and Thomas McCormick, have questioned Pratt's thesis, finding it contradicted by substantial evidence and too reliant upon business journals rather than upon the actions and ideas of businessmen and companies, an important number of whom saw domestic prosperity dependent upon expansion into foreign markets. Then, too, if American business was as influential, as most agree it was, in the domestic development of America after the Civil War, can we easily deny, as Pratt does, that it lacked influence in foreign policy? Were businessmen economic expansionists only at home?

On the other hand, Thomas J. McCormick, like LaFeber, finds economic questions at the forefront. Government, military, and business leaders joined to articulate a case for colonies as stepping stones to the anticipated rich markets of China. McCormick is emphatic in denying that irrational factors explain American behavior. American imperialism, he argues, derived from a conscious thirst for foreign economic expansion and the conviction that areas like the Philippines were needed, not as traditional colonies, but as way stations to the more valuable Chinese marketplace. McCormick places decision-making power in an elite, with McKinley as an active member, which sought foreign outlets for domestic surplus production and which looked happily upon the Spanish-American War as a chance to fulfill the elite's objective. McCormick and Pratt agree that American businessmen had an intense interest in the China market, but at what point do these authors disagree? How do they depict the political process? How does China figure in American imperialism?

William Appleman Williams (*The Tragedy of American Diplomacy* [1962]) was one of the first post-World War II historians to question Pratt's thesis. Williams argued that elite American commercial interests, in alliance with willing government leaders sharing a vision of economic opportunity abroad, carried America into empire consciously and deliberately. However, in his latest work, *The Roots of the Modern American Empire* (1968), Williams concludes that American imperialism in the late nineteenth century originated in the rational thinking of American farmers—a majority of "the people"—who eventually convinced commercial interests that a foreign marketplace was essential to American prosperity. It was a people's war and a people's economic imperialism, but neither was prompted by hysteria or irrationality. Does Williams's new theme, as some scholars have claimed, ignore too many other factors?

Ernest R. May attempts a synthesis of interpretations by suggesting that all the motives, whether economic, humanitarian, nationalistic, Social Darwinist, or psychic, were at work. The important question for him is: What process allowed these motives to be expressed and acted upon? May speculates that European publicists temporarily dissuaded an American foreign policy elite from its previous anti-imperialist stance. But after the colonial spurt, May tells us, the elite returned to its anti-imperialist ways and took the American people with them. May concludes that the impetus for imperialism came from abroad. Is it true that American imperialism was not derived from an *American* calculation of its national interest and hence was essentially mindless? May concluded in an earlier book (*Imperial Democracy* [1961]) that the United States "had greatness thrust upon it" after 1895, and that American leaders "were at most only incidentally concerned about real or imagined interests abroad." Were American leaders so unconcerned? Were they so passive? And importantly, what is May's definition of imperialism? Did America discontinue its "career as an imperial power" after 1900?

The anti-imperialists who lost the debate of the 1890s answered in the negative. The anti-imperialist movement included such prominent Americans as steel magnate Andrew Carnegie; Samuel Gompers, president of the American Federation of Labor; Social Darwinist William Graham Sumner; agrarian representative William Jennings Bryan; and Mark Twain, unmatched humorist and satirist. With such influential leadership, why did the anti-imperialists fail? In the Philippines, the anti-imperialists had established a viable government led by a popular leader, Emilio Aguinaldo. Why did they fail? The selections that follow attempt answers.

Robert L. Beisner, in *Twelve Against Empire* (1968), emphasizes an important element of the American anti-imperialist movement—the mugwumps, who organized the Anti-Imperialist League. As previous selections have noted, many imperialists derived their foreign-policy positions from domestic concerns, such as social unrest or glutted markets. What domestic influences affected the foreign policy ideas of the anti-imperialists? Beisner finds them late in organizing and weak from internal schism, but essentially applauds them for alerting Americans to the unfortunate consequences of imperialist conduct. He poses an interpretive problem: Were the anti-imperialists themselves at fault for losing the debate or were they faced with irreversible *faits accomplis* (actual American possession of foreign territories after the war) by the McKinley administration, against which they were helpless? Which men, the anti-imperialists or imperialists, adhered most closely to "traditional" American principles and foreign policy?

Beisner notes that many anti-imperialists were racists. Beale has depicted Roosevelt and other imperialists as racists, too. Christopher Lasch goes much further and argues that the debate between the two camps was insignificant because both believed in the inequality of man and racial superiority. Definition is again important: Is the "central assumption of imperialism" the "natural inequality of man," as Lasch asserts? Which anti-imperialists does Lasch use in his evidence? Were there *no* differences between the racism of the imperialists and the racism of their opponents? Lasch sharply chastises the anti-imperialists for abandoning both the Filipinos and the American blacks. Does Lasch mean that the anti-imperialists should have sought to annex the Philippines to help the Filipinos in their quest for self-government, rather than abandon them to the imperialists? Or is Lasch's interpretation "a plague on both your houses"?

Claiming that Lasch had defined the problem too narrowly and had looked only at a segment of the anti-imperialist group, Richard E. Welch, Jr., studies a wide spectrum of anti-imperialists in his selection. How does Welch argue that racism does not explain anti-imperialism? And what distinctions does he make in arguing against other scholars who have claimed that both groups in the debate were economic expansionists and therefore in slight disagreement? The debate over empire was not mere shadowboxing, not mere rhetoric, according to Welch, but one of substance about the basic nature and mission of the United States.

Seldom have American historians given much attention to anti-imperialism in the Philippines or to the scholarship of Filipinos. The Spanish-American War receives dramatic attention; but the bloody Filipino Insurrection, which began against Spain in 1896 and lasted until mid-1902 against the United States is slighted. To be sure, it is an ugly episode in the history of American foreign relations, and until recently American scholars have tended to play down the sordid side of United States history. But in the Philippines, Teodoro A. Agoncillo has long stressed his people's struggle for independence against the United States. He is critical of Americans for snubbing Aguinaldo's nationalist government and for misleading Filipinos to think that they would soon be masters of their own land. But Agoncillo also criticizes the intellectual-business elite in the Philippines for settling for less than independence. Agoncillo asks an intriguing question: What if Aguinaldo, instead of trusting the Americans and cooling his military advisers, had attacked the Americans early when they were still numerically weak? We can suggest after reading Agoncillo, other Filipinos, and Cuban nationalists (who emphasize their revolution against Spain in the 1870s and 1895–1898) that the Spanish-American War might be renamed the "Cuban-Filipino-Spanish-American War." Such a name would more accurately identify the combatants, recognize where the war was fought, and clarify whose interests were primarily involved.

Running through most of the literature on American imperialism and anti-imperialism in the 1890s, but especially after the beginning of the Spanish-American War, is the theme that the United States could not have done otherwise. That is, for example, that McKinley had no choice but to annex the Philippines. As Beisner has written: "It is the virtually unanimous judgment of diplomatic historians that there was no politic way to get out of the Philippines after Dewey's naval victory of May 1, 1898." From reference to the Philippines alone, historians often move to the entire American imperialist record and give to it an interpretation of inevitability as well. If we accept the inevitability of American imperialism, do not the anti-imperialist alternatives and arguments (no colonies or protectorate status, for example) seem irrelevant? Yet few scholars would dismiss the anti-imperialist critique as irrelevant. We should consider, then, the alternatives and options open to, but rejected by, the McKinley administration, and question any interpretation hinting inexorability. A notion of inevitability for the Philippines does not help us understand why the United States took Guam, Hawaii, and Puerto Rico and intruded into the sovereignty of Latin America. But our identification of alternatives will help us explain why the McKinley administration and the imperialists made the decisions they did, for they had to justify their rejection of the alternatives. With a study of both the decisions and the rejected alternatives, we can answer not only the question "What happened?" but also that of "What went wrong?"

part one
imperialism: the spanish-american war and empire

one
the preparation

WALTER LaFEBER

*Walter LaFeber (b. 1933), professor of history at Cornell
University, has distinguished himself as a diplomatic
historian.* The New Empire *(1963), from which the
following selection is chosen, won the Albert J. Beveridge
Award from the American Historical Association in 1962. A
student of William A. Williams at the University of
Wisconsin, LaFeber, like his mentor, has emphasized the
important role of the "open-door" philosophy in American
foreign relations—a philosophy growing out of domestic
economic developments. His well-received* America, Russia,
and the Cold War, 1945–1966 *(1967) continues this
theme, as well as the interpretation that American leaders
have been conscious formulators of an expansionist foreign
policy.*

Modern American diplomatic history began in the 1850's
and 1860's. By then the continental empire of which
Madison, Jefferson, and John Quincy Adams had dreamed
spanned North America from sea to sea. Cords of rails
and water, common economic and social interests, and a
federal political system tied the empire together. Edmund
Burke had stated the principle: "An empire is the aggregate
of many states under one common head, whether this
head be a monarch or a presiding republic."

But by the time William Seward became Lincoln's
Secretary of State in 1861, a new empire had started to
take form. Two important features distinguished it from
the old. First, with the completion of the continental
conquest Americans moved with increasing authority into
such extracontinental areas as Hawaii, Latin America, Asia,
and Africa. Second, the form of expansion changed.

Source: *The New Empire: An Interpretation of American
Expansion, 1860–1898* (Ithaca, N.Y.: Cornell University Press,
1963), pp. 1–3, 4–5, 24–32. Copyright © 1963 by the American
Historical Association. Used by permission of Cornell University
Press.

Instead of searching for farming, mineral, or grazing lands, Americans sought foreign markets for agricultural staples or industrial goods. In the late 1840's America export figures began their rapid climb to the dizzying heights of the twentieth century. Between 1850 and 1873, despite an almost nonexistent export trade during the Civil War, exports averaged $274,000,000 annually; the yearly average during the 1838–1849 period had been only $116,000,000.

As these figures indicate, the United States was not isolated from the rest of the world in the years 1850–1873. When examined in economic and ideological terms, the familiar story of American isolation becomes a myth. It is true, however, that from the end of the Napoleonic Wars until the 1890's the vast Atlantic sheltered America from many European problems. Many problems, but not all, for even before the 1890's the United States became involved in such episodes as the international slave trade, Latin-American revolutions, numerous incidents in Asia with the major powers of the world, and even colonial questions in Africa and Madagascar.

External factors, such as England's command of the seas and the balance of power in Europe, might have given the United States the luxury of almost total isolation; but internal developments, as interpreted by American policy makers, led the United States to become increasingly involved in world affairs. The economic revolution, new scientific and ideological concepts, and the policy makers' views of these changes had begun to accelerate this involvement before the Civil War.

This development is sometimes overlooked, since economic and ideological expansion are often considered apart from political entanglements. American history, of course, belies such a separation, for the United States annexed a continental empire by undermining, economically and ideologically, British, French, Spanish, Mexican, and Indian control and then taking final possession with money, bullets, or both. Similarly, one rule may be suggested which particularly helps in understanding the course of American foreign policy in the nineteenth century: the United States could not obtain either continental or overseas economic benefits without paying a political and often a military price. Economic expansion and political involvement became so interlinked that by 1900 a reinvigorated Monroe Doctrine, participation in an increasing number of international conferences, and a magnificent battleship fleet necessarily made explicit America's worldwide political commitments. . . .

Long before the 1860's Americans had been involved in the affairs of Canada, Latin America, Hawaii, and Asia. In its first moments of independence, the United States had struck quickly and unsuccessfully in an effort to bring into the new nation the territory north and east of the Great Lakes. The Americans failed no less miserably in their second try during the War of 1812. But two strikes were not out, and time and again in the first half of the nineteenth century Americans tried more subtle measures for adding Canada to the Union. The carrot of trade replaced the stick of war when in 1854 the United States and Canada entered into a reciprocity treaty which many Americans hoped would tie the northern nation to them with unbreakable economic bonds. When the treaty tended instead to strengthen Canadian autonomy, a disgusted American Senate allowed the agreement to terminate in 1866.

The United States did not attempt to annex Latin America as it did Canada, but there was no lack of interest in the southern continent. Jefferson had declared that North America would be the nest from which the entire Western Hemisphere would be peopled. Henry Clay later admonished the United States to put itself at the head of the entire hemisphere through a "Good Neighborhood" policy. Increasing interest in Latin-American markets as replacements for those lost with the closing of the Napoleonic Wars in Europe provided adequate material reasons. In a negative sense, the Monroe Doctrine, as formulated by President James Monroe and Secretary of State John Quincy Adams, had tried to exclude European powers from affairs in this hemisphere. Viewed positively, the Doctrine staked out the hemisphere as an area for future American economic opportunity and *de facto* political control. In the mid-1890's an American Secretary of State would announce the positive aspects of the Doctrine in blunt terms. The annexation of Texas in 1845, which had formerly been a part of Mexico, the war with Mexico in 1846–1848, which resulted in the enlargement of the United States by one-fifth, and the numerous filibustering expeditions into Central America in the 1850's only partially indicated American interest in lands south of the border.

Also to the south lay Cuba, an island which Jefferson had considered annexing as early as 1808 and which John Quincy Adams delayed taking only because he believed that the "laws of political . . . gravitation" demanded that Cuba, like "an apple, severed by the tempest from its native tree," would "gravitate only towards the North American Union." By the 1850's Cuba had refused to fall in spite of increased American interest, so three distinguished United States envoys to Europe decided to shake the tree. Failing to persuade Spain to sell the island, they issued the Ostend Manifesto, which proclaimed the right of the United States to take the island if Spain would not sell it. Washington, however, quickly disavowed the Manifesto. Such expansionist projects failed in the 1850's, not because they were unpopular, but because too many of them were advocated by men who spoke with the drawl of southern slaveholders. Even such northern expansionists as Seward refused to cooperate in attempts to extend the slavocracy.

American attention had also turned to the Pacific. Trading and whaling vessels from Massachusetts had early stamped the Hawaiian Islands as outposts of United States trade. New England missionaries established colonies during the 1820's. Soon American interests grew from within as well as from without. In the 1840's the United States began sending notices to England and France (the mailing list would later include Germany and Japan) that it would not tolerate European control of the islands. By the decade before the Civil War, the American Secretary of State, William L. Marcy, tried to negotiate a treaty of annexation with Hawaii, was outsmarted by the antiannexationist bloc in Honolulu, and retreated with the warning that future annexation by the United States was "inevitable." More than forty years later William McKinley would say, while successfully annexing the islands, that his action was "the inevitable consequence" of "three-quarters of a century" of American expansion into the Pacific.

By the time of the Civil War, the Monroe Doctrine had been implicitly extended as far as Hawaii, but important American interests were developing still farther west. (Textbooks call the Orient the Far East, but this hinders the understanding of American expansion, for the United States has more often considered this area as the Far West.) The "Empress of China" had sailed out of New York City in 1784 to make the first important contact. The United States signed its first commercial treaty with China in 1844. Ten years later Commodore Matthew C. Perry opened Japan. By the time Seward assumed his duties as Secretary of State, the United States had been caught in the web of Asian power politics. The State Department had to maintain trade privileges and safeguard traders and missionaries either by cooperating with the European powers or by developing a go-it-alone policy. Americans debated only the means, not the fact of involvement.

* * *

In the unfolding drama of the new empire William Henry Seward appears as the prince of players. Grant, Hamilton Fish, William M. Evarts, James G. Blaine, Frederick T. Frelinghuysen, and Thomas F. Bayard assume secondary roles. Although Seward left the stage in the first act of the drama, only a few of the other players could improve on his techniques, and none could approach his vision of American empire.

Henry Adams described Seward near the end of his career as "a slouching, slender figure; a head like a wise macaw; a beaked nose; shaggy eyebrows; unorderly hair and clothes; hoarse voice; offhand manner; free talk, and perpetual cigar." Seward nevertheless attracted an urbane, educated person like young Adams, for the Secretary of State, like Adams, was an intellectual in nearly every sense of the word. He won Phi Beta Kappa honors at Union College while still in his teens and for a short time taught school. His son later noted that Seward regularly read Chaucer, Spenser, Ben Jonson, Ariosto, Macaulay, Carlyle, Burke, Lieber, and Prescott's histories "as fast as they came out." He also knew the Latin classics, but his favorite, appropriately enough, was the theorist of the British Empire, Francis Bacon. Seward also learned from John Quincy Adams. It was not coincidental that Seward's ideas of American empire so resembled those of Adams; after Adams' death, Seward eulogized, "I have lost a patron, a guide, a counsellor, and a friend—one whom I loved scarcely less than the dearest relations, and venerated above all that was mortal among men."

He also understood more mundane things—such as the value of political parties for his own advancement. When once asked how to fight slavery he answered: "Organization! Organization! Nothing but organization." This served as the motto for most of his political operations. He was tabbed by many political observers as the Republican nominee for the White House in 1860. But paradoxically, he was cut off from the strongest segments of the

Republican party during the 1865–1869 period, the years when he most
actively worked for the advancement of the new empire.

Seward deserves to be remembered as the greatest Secretary of State in
American history after his beloved Adams. This is so partially because of his
astute diplomacy, which kept European powers out of the Civil War, but
also because his vision of empire dominated American policy for the next
century. He based this vision, as would be expected of an intellectual, on "a
political law—and when I say political law, I mean a higher law, a law of
Providence—that empire has, for the last three thousand years . . . made
its way constantly westward, and that it must continue to move on westward
until the tides of the renewed and of the decaying civilizations of the world
meet on the shores of the Pacific Ocean." In the same speech he noted,
"Empire moves far more rapidly in modern than it did in ancient times."
In this single pronouncement, noting the historic movement of empire westward
across America and into the Pacific and Asia, Seward anticipated many
(especially Brooks Adams) who would ring the changes on this theme in the
1890's; he emphasized that this imperial movement traveled at a much faster
speed during an industrial age than it did in ancient times; and he reiterated the
theme of imperial manifest destiny ordained by Providence for the American
people.

Seward spent much of his life attempting to prepare the United States
for its proper role in this westward flight of empire. It was his misfortune that
he tried to unify and strengthen the nation for this role at the very time
slavery made his task impossible. After the Civil War he renewed his quest.
He always envisioned an empire which would not be acquired haphazardly,
but would develop along carefully worked out lines. The best word to
describe his concept of empire, perhaps, is integrated. The empire would begin
with a strong, consolidated base of power on the American continent and
move into the way stations of the Pacific as it approached the final goal of Asia.
Each area would have its own functions to perform and become an integrated
part of the whole empire.

Seward prophesied that the battle for world power would occur in Asia,
since "commerce has brought the ancient continents near to us." But the victor
in this battle would be the nation operating from the strongest economic and
power base. Therefore he advised in 1853:

*Open up a highway through your country from New York to San
Francisco. Put your domain under cultivation, and your ten
thousand wheels of manufacture in motion. Multiply your ships, and
send them forth to the East. The nation that draws most materials
and provisions from the earth, and fabricates the most, and sells the most
of productions and fabrics to foreign nations, must be, and will be,
the great power of the earth.*

Seward offered concrete suggestions to realize this base of power. First, he
advised the passing of a high tariff to protect small industries and attract foreign
laborers. Once Europe was drained of her cheap labor, the ocean could be

6

"reduced to a ferry" for American products. High tariffs would also allow effective planning and allocation of resources by the federal government and give the government money for internal improvements (an idea from John Quincy Adams' repertoire). Second, Seward wanted to offer the public lands quickly and at low prices. This would not only attract cheap labor, but would also provide adequate agricultural products; "commercial supremacy demands just such an agricultural basis" as American lands, when inhabited, could supply. Third, he hoped to obtain cheap labor, especially by enticing Asian workers. He accomplished this with the 1868 treaty between the United States and China, which gave Chinese laborers almost unrestricted entry into the country. Finally, he would tie the continent together with canals and one or more transcontinental railroads. Money was no object: "It is necessary; and since it is necessary, there is the end of the argument." Seward summed up these views with a favorite story of the barbarian looking at King Croesus' great hoard of gold and then remarking: "It is all very well; but whoever comes upon you with better iron than you have, will be master of all this gold." Seward would add: "We shall find it so in the end."

Latin America and Canada would inevitably become a part of this continental base. Seward declared that he wanted no American colonies in Latin America, but this did not mean he found no interest in the area. He feared that establishing colonies would result in either a standing army in the United States or anarchy in the colonies. Instead, he wanted to hold islands in the Caribbean which would serve as strategic bases to protect an Isthmian route to the Pacific and also prevent European powers from dabbling in the area of the North American coastline. But Central America would come into the Union eventually when "the ever-increasing expansion of the American people westward and southward" began. Soon Mexico would "be opening herself as cheerfully to American immigration as Montana and Idaho are now." Then Mexico would not be a colony, but a state, fulfilling Seward's prophecy that Mexico City was an excellent site for the future capital of the American empire. Canada would also eventually be a part of the continental base. In an 1860 speech Seward noted that "an ingenious, enterprising, and ambitious people" are building Canada, "and I am able to say, 'It is very well, you are building excellent states to be hereafter admitted into the American Union.' "

In the same speech he made a similar comment about Alaska. Seward realized this particular dream when he negotiated its purchase in 1867. The United States bought "Seward's Icebox" for several good reasons, including traditional American friendship for Russia, the hope that the deal would sandwich British Columbia between American territory and make inevitable its annexation, and the belief that Alaskan resources would more than pay the $7,200,000 price tag. But given Seward's view of empire, perhaps his son, a distinguished diplomat in his own right, later offered the best reason: "To the United States, it would give a foothold for commercial and naval operations accessible from the Pacific States." Nathaniel P. Banks, Chairman of the House Foreign Affairs Committee in 1867 and a strong supporter of Seward's imperial ideas, called the Aleutians the "drawbridge between America and Asia."

Seward approached the Asian market cautiously and methodically. Alaska protected one flank. An American-controlled canal would provide a southern corridor. In the center would be California and Hawaii. California, Seward exulted:

California that comes from the clime where the west dies away into the rising east; California, that bounds at once the empire and the continent; California, the youthful queen of the Pacific. . . . The world contains no seat of empire so magnificent as this. . . . The nation thus situated . . . must command the empire of the seas, which alone is real empire.

Hawaii offered the next step west. Here Seward promoted the American representative to Minister Resident in 1863 and four years later tried to prepare the islands for the hug of annexation by pulling Hawaii into a reciprocity treaty. The Senate was too busy with Reconstruction to deal with Seward's proposal, but he nevertheless told the American Minister in September, 1867, that annexation was still "deemed desirable by this government." He was immediately successful in placing the Stars and Stripes above the Midway islands in 1867. These islands, 1,200 miles west of Hawaii, became an important outpost for America's Pacific interests.

And beyond lay the bottomless markets of Asia, "the prize" for which Europe and the United States contended, "the chief theatre of events in the world's great hereafter." Here lay the crucial area if the United States hoped to control "the commerce of the world, which is the empire of the world." Here too the United States moving westward would meet another great nation moving eastward. "Russia and the United States," the new Secretary of State wrote to the American Minister to Russia in May, 1861, "may remain good friends until, each having made a circuit of half the globe in opposite directions, they shall meet and greet each other in the region where civilization first began." Seward had few illusions about the implications of his expansionist policy.

America's success in Asia depended upon the success of its open-door policy, which advocated equal commercial rights for all nations and no territorial aggrandizement by any. Seward cooperated with European powers in order to protect this American policy. The open-door concept was nothing new, dating back to the most-favored-nation clauses in the first American-Chinese treaty in 1844. What was new was Seward's vigorous moves to protect the policy. He could deal gently with China; the Burlingame Treaty of 1868 provided for the preservation of American rights of travel and residence in China as well as freer entry into the United States for Chinese laborers. But the Secretary of State was tough with Japan. When that nation proved reluctant to correct what Seward considered to be infringements upon American rights, he ordered naval units to participate in a show of strength that climaxed with the powers dictating to Japan from a British gunboat. He was equally vigorous in Korea. At one point he proposed to the French that they cooperate with the United States to force open the Hermit Kingdom to outside interests. When the French refused this offer, Seward sent his nephew, George F. Seward, to sign a trade treaty with Korea, but this attempt also failed. Fifteen years later, however, Korea grudgingly opened its doors to American traders and missionaries.

Henry Adams summed it up: "The policy of Mr. Seward was based upon this fixed idea [of expansion], which, under his active direction, assumed a development that even went somewhat too far and too fast for the public." Seward's Caribbean plans, especially the purchase of the Danish West Indies and Santo Domingo, came to nothing. Nor did he bring Hawaii into the American orbit when he wanted. But he did outline in some detail his ideas of an integrated empire with a great continental base which would produce vast quantities of goods for hundreds of millions of consumers in Asia. He did see the completion of the transcontinental railroad, industries supported by tariffs and internal improvements, and the acquisition of Alaska and Midway as way stations to the Asian market. He accomplished much of his work, moreover, despite the Civil War and a strong antiexpansionist feeling in the late 1860's.

The antiexpansionists effectively used several arguments to thwart Seward's ambitions. As noted earlier, they claimed that the United States suffered from a land glut already; no more land could properly be developed. If the Union acquired more territory, it might be Latin-American, and this would aggravate the race problem. Others argued that the United States should avoid a colonial policy, especially at a time when England was trying to dispose of her own unprofitable outlying areas. Finally, some antiexpansionists urged financial retrenchment in order to start American industries and farms booming again rather than paying fancy price tags for noncontiguous territory. The most notable characteristic of these arguments is not that they were effective in the late 1860's, but that they melted away in large measure after the 1870's, as the frontier closed, an open-door commercial policy eliminated colonial problems, and American factories and farms boomed so successfully that the resulting glut of goods threatened to inundate the economy. With these changes, Seward's successors were able to complete much of what he had been unable to finish.

two
the people's
war

WILLIAM E. LEUCHTENBURG

*This selection appeared in 1957, before Margaret Leech and
H. Wayne Morgan, among others, wrote books arguing
that President William McKinley had been a strong leader,
not buffeted easily by the winds of public opinion, and
not manipulated by advisers. William E. Leuchtenburg
(b. 1922) did not have the benefit of these studies, and his
essay reflects the then-current historical interpretation
of McKinley as an indecisive leader who did not lead. He
also treats the war as an expression of popular American
hunger for foreign ventures built up over a period of
years, and unlike LaFeber, Leuchtenburg stresses
the impact of irrational and emotional factors in foreign
policy. A professor of history at Columbia University,
where he has taught since 1952, Leuchtenburg has written
on a variety of recent historical topics, but his scholarship
has centered lately on the presidential leadership of
Franklin D. Roosevelt. His* Flood Control Politics *(1953),*
Perils of Prosperity, 1914–1932 *(1958), and* Franklin D.
Roosevelt and the New Deal, 1932–1940 *(1963) reflect
wide research and a flair for interesting reporting.*

The United States in the 1890's became more aggressive,
expansionistic, and jingoistic than it had been since
the 1850's. In less than five years, we came to the brink of
war with Italy, Chile, and Great Britain over three minor
incidents in which no American national interest of major
importance was involved. In each of these incidents,

Source: William E. Leuchtenburg, "The Needless War with
Spain," *American Heritage* 8 (February 1957): 33–41, 95.
Copyright © 1957 by American Heritage Publishing Co., Inc.
Reprinted by permission from the February 1957 issue of *American
Heritage* magazine.

our secretary of state was highly aggressive, and the American people applauded. During these years, we completely overhauled our decrepit Navy, building fine new warships like the *Maine*. The martial virtues of Napoleon, the imperial doctrines of Rudyard Kipling, and the naval theories of Captain Alfred T. Mahan all enjoyed a considerable vogue.

There was an apparently insatiable hunger for foreign conquest. Senator Shelby M. Cullom declared in 1895: "It is time that some one woke up and realized the necessity of annexing some property. We want all this northern hemisphere, and when we begin to reach out to secure these advantages we will begin to have a nation and our lawmakers will rise above the grade of politicians and become true statesmen." When, in 1895, the United States almost became involved in a war with Great Britain over the Venezuelan boundary, Theodore Roosevelt noted: "The antics of the bankers, brokers and anglo-maniacs generally are humiliating to a degree. . . . Personally I rather hope the fight will come soon. The clamor of the peace faction has convinced me that this country needs a war." The Washington *Post* concluded: "The taste of Empire is in the mouth of the people. . . ."

In the early nineteenth century, under the leadership of men like Simon Bolivar, Spain's colonies in the New World had launched a series of successful revolutions; of the great Spanish empire that Cortes and Pizarro had built, the island of Cuba, "the Ever Faithful Isle," was the only important Spanish possession to stay loyal to the Crown. Spain exploited the economy of the island mercilessly, forcing Cubans to buy Spanish goods at prices far above the world market, and Madrid sent to Cuba as colonial officials younger sons who had no interest in the island other than making a quick killing and returning to Spain. High taxes to support Spanish officialdom crippled the island; arbitrary arrests and arbitrary trials made a mockery of justice; and every attempt at public education was stifled.

The island of Cuba had been in a state of political turbulence for years when in 1894 the American Wilson-Gorman Tariff placed duties on Cuban sugar which, coupled with a world-wide depression, brought ruin to the economy of the island. The terrible hardship of the winter was the signal for revolution; on February 24, 1895, under the leadership of a junta in New York City headed by José Martí, rebels once more took the field against Spain. At first, the American people were too absorbed with the Venezuelan crisis to pay much attention to another revolt in Cuba. Then, in September, 1895, came the event which changed the course of the Cuban rebellion: William Randolph Hearst, a young man of 32 who had been operating the San Francisco *Examiner* in a sensational fashion, purchased the New York *Morning Journal,* and immediately locked horns with Joseph Pulitzer and the *World* in a circulation war that was to make newspaper history.

Hearst capitalized on the fact that the American people had only the most romantic notions of the nature of the Cuban conflict. The rebels under General Máximo Gómez, a tough Santo Domingan guerrilla fighter, embarked on a program of burning the cane fields in the hope not only of depriving the government of revenue but also of so disrupting the life of the island that the government would be forced to submit. Although there were some noble spirits in the group, much of the rebellion had an unsavory odor; one of the main financial supports for the uprising came from American property owners who feared that their sugar fields would be burned unless protection money was paid.

While Gómez was putting Cuba to the torch, American newsmen were filing reports describing the war in terms of nonexistent pitched battles between the liberty-loving Cubans and the cruel Spaniards. The war was presented, in short, as a Byronic conflict between the forces of freedom and the forces of tyranny, and the American people ate it up. When Hearst bought the *Journal* in late 1895, it had a circulation of 30,000; by 1897 it had bounded to over 400,000 daily, and during the Spanish-American War it was to go well over a million.

The sensational newspapers had influence, yet they represented no more than a minority of the press of the country; and in the South and the Middle West, where anti-Spanish feeling became most intense, the representative newspaper was much more conservative. Certainly the yellow press played a tremendous part in whipping up sentiment for intervention in Cuba, but these feelings could not be carried into action unless American political leaders of both parties were willing to assume the terrible responsibility of war.

By the beginning of 1896 the rebels had achieved such success in their guerrilla tactics that Madrid decided on firmer steps and sent General Don Valeriano Weyler y Nicolau to Cuba. When Weyler arrived in February, he found the sugar industry severely disrupted and the military at a loss to meet the rebel tactic of setting fire to the cane fields. Weyler declared martial law and announced that men guilty of incendiarism would be dealt with summarily; he was promptly dubbed "The Butcher" by American newspapermen.

By late 1896 Weyler still had not succeeded in crushing the insurrection, and his measures became more severe. On October 21 he issued his famous *reconcentrado* order, directing the "reconcentration" of the people of Pinar del Río in the garrison towns, and forbidding the exports of supplies from the towns to the countryside. Reasoning that he could never suppress the rebellion so long as the rebels could draw secret assistance from people in the fields, Weyler moved the people from the estates into the towns and stripped the countryside of supplies to starve out the rebellion. Since many of the people had already fled to the towns, the *reconcentrado* policy was not as drastic as it appeared; yet the suffering produced by the policy was undeniable. Lacking proper hygienic care, thousands of Cubans, especially women and children, died like flies.

When William McKinley entered the White House in 1897, he had no intention of joining the War Hawks. "If I can only go out of office . . . with the knowledge that I have done what lay in my power to avert this terrible calamity," McKinley told Grover Cleveland on the eve of his inauguration, "I shall be the happiest man in the world." McKinley came to power as the "advance agent of prosperity," and business interests were almost unanimous in opposing any agitation of the Cuban question that might lead to war. Contrary to the assumptions of Leninist historians, it was Wall Street which, first and last, resisted a war which was to bring America its overseas empire.

The country had been gripped since 1893 by the deepest industrial depression in its history, a depression that was to persist until the beginning of 1897. Each time it appeared recovery might be on its way, a national crisis had cut it off: first the Venezuelan boundary war scare of December, 1895, then the bitter free silver campaign of 1896. What business groups feared more than anything else was a new crisis. As Julius Pratt writes: "To this fair prospect of a great business revival the threat of war was like a specter at the feast."

McKinley was not a strong President, and he had no intention of being one. Of all the political figures of his day, he was the man most responsive to the popular will. It was his great virtue and, his critics declared, his great weakness. Uncle Joe Cannon once remarked: "McKinley keeps his ear to the ground so close that he gets it full of grasshoppers much of the time." If McKinley was not one of our greatest Presidents, he was certainly the most representative and the most responsive. Anyone who knew the man knew that, although he was strongly opposed to war, he would not hold out against war if the popular demand for war became unmistakable. "Let the voice of the people rule"—this was McKinley's credo, and he meant it.

The threat to peace came from a new quarter, from the South and West, the strongholds of Democracy and free silver. Many Bryanite leaders were convinced that a war would create such a strain on the currency system that the opposition to free silver would collapse. Moreover, with the opposition to war strongest in Wall Street, they found it easy to believe that Administration policy was the product of a conspiracy of bankers who would deny silver to the American people, who would deny liberty to the people of Cuba, who were concerned only with the morality of the countinghouse. Moreover, Bryan was the spokesman for rural Protestantism, which was already speaking in terms of a righteous war against Spain to free the Cubans from bondage. These were forces too powerful for McKinley to ignore. McKinley desired peace, but he was above all, a Republican partisan, and he had no intention of handing the Democrats in 1900 the campaign cry of Free Cuba and Free Silver.

While McKinley attempted to search out a policy that would preserve peace without bringing disaster to the Republican party, the yellow press made his job all the more difficult by whipping up popular anger against Spain. On February 12 the *Journal* published a dispatch from Richard Harding Davis, reporting that as the American steamship *Olivette* was about to leave Havana Harbor for the United States, it was boarded by Spanish police officers who searched three young Cuban women, one of whom was suspected of carrying messages from the rebels. The *Journal* ran the story under the headline, "Does Our Flag Protect Women?" with a vivid drawing by Frederic Remington across one half a page showing Spanish plainclothesmen searching a wholly nude woman. War, declared the *Journal,* "is a dreadful thing, but there are things more dreadful than even war, and one of them is dishonor." It shocked the country, and Congressman Amos Cummings immediately resolved to launch a congressional inquiry into the *Olivette* outrage. Before any steps could be taken, the true story was revealed. The *World* produced one of the young women who indignantly protested the *Journal*'s version of the incident. Pressured by the *World,* the *Journal* was forced to print a letter from Davis explaining that his article had not said that male policemen had searched the women and that, in fact, the search had been conducted quite properly by a police matron with no men present.

The *Olivette* incident was manufactured by Hearst, but by the spring of 1897 the American press had a new horror to report which was all too true. Famine was stalking the island. Cuba had been in a serious economic state when the rebellion broke out in 1895; two years of war would, under any circumstances, have been disastrous, but the deliberate policies pursued both by the insurgents and by the government forces made the situation desperate. It was a simple matter for Hearst and Pulitzer reporters to pin the full responsibility on Weyler.

By the middle of July, McKinley had formulated a policy which he set down in a letter of instructions to our new American minister to Spain, General Stewart L. Woodford. The letter emphasized the need of bringing the Cuban war to an end and said that this could be done to the mutual advantage of both Spain and the Cubans by granting some kind of autonomy to Cuba. If Spain did not make an offer to the rebels and if the "measures of unparalleled severity" were not ended, the United States threatened to intervene.

On August 8 an Italian anarchist assassinated the Spanish premier; and when Woodford reached Madrid in September, a new government was about to take over headed by Señor Sagasta and the Liberals, who had repeatedly denounced the "barbarity" of the previous government's policy in Cuba. Sagasta immediately removed General Weyler, and the prospects for an agreement between the United States and Spain took a decided turn for the better.

While Woodford was carrying on skillful diplomatic negotiations for peace in Madrid, the Hearst press was creating a new sensation in this country with the Cisneros affair. Evangelina Cisneros was a young Cuban woman who had been arrested and imprisoned in the Rocojidas in Havana, guilty, according to the American press, of no other crime than protecting her virtue from an unscrupulous Spanish colonel, an aide to Butcher Weyler. The Rocojidas, Hearst's reporter told American readers, was a cage where the innocent beauty was herded with women criminals of every type, subject to the taunts and vile invitations of men who gathered outside.

When it was reported that Señorita Cisneros, whose father was a rebel leader, was to be sent for a long term to a Spanish penal colony in Africa or in the Canaries, the *Journal* launched one of the most fabulous campaigns in newspaper history. "Enlist the women of America!" was the Hearst war cry, and the women of America proved willing recruits. Mrs. Julia Ward Howe signed an appeal to Pope Leo XIII, and Mrs. Jefferson Davis, the widow of the president of the Confederacy, appealed to the queen regent of Spain to "give Evangelina Cisneros to the women of America to save her from a fate worse than death." When the *Journal* prepared a petition on behalf of Señorita Cisneros, it obtained the names of Mrs. Nancy McKinley, the mother of the President, and Mrs. John Sherman, the wife of the secretary of state, as well as such other prominent ladies as Julia Dent Grant and Mrs. Mark Hanna.

It was a startling coup for Mr. Hearst, but he had not yet even begun to display his ingenuity. On October 10, 1897, the *Journal* erupted across its front

page with the banner headline: "An American Newspaper Accomplishes at a
Single Stroke What the Best Efforts of Diplomacy Failed Utterly to Bring
About in Many Months." Hearst had sent Karl Decker, one of his most reliable
correspondents, to Havana in late August with orders to rescue the Cuban
Girl Martyr "at any hazard"; and Decker had climbed to the roof of a house
near the prison, broken the bar of a window of the jail, lifted Evangelina out,
and, after hiding her for a few days in Havana, smuggled her onto an
American steamer. Decker, signing his dispatch to the *Journal* "Charles Duval,"
wrote: "I have broken the bars of Rocojidas and have set free the beautiful
captive of monster Weyler. Weyler could blind the Queen to the real character
of Evangelina, but he could not build a jail that would hold against *Journal*
enterprise when properly set to work." The Cuban Girl Martyr was met at
the pier by a great throng, led up Broadway in a triumphal procession, taken
to a reception at Delmonico's where 120,000 people milled about the
streets surrounding the restaurant, and hailed at a monster reception in
Madison Square Garden. The Bishop of London cabled his congratulations
to the *Journal,* while Governor Stephens of Missouri proposed that the *Journal*
send down 500 of its reporters to free the entire island.

On October 23 Sagasta announced a "total change of immense scope" in
Spanish policy in Cuba. He promised to grant local autonomy to the Cubans
immediately, reserving justice, the armed forces, and foreign relations to Spain.
On November 13 Weyler's successor, Captain-General Blanco, issued a decree
modifying considerably the *reconcentrado* policy, and on November 25 the
queen regent signed the edicts creating an autonomous government for
the island. In essence, Madrid had acceded to the American demands.

While Woodford was conducting negotiations with a conciliatory Liberal
government in Madrid and while there was still hope for peace, the fatal
incident occurred which made war virtually inevitable. On January 12, 1898,
a riot broke out in Havana, and Spanish officers attacked newspaper offices. The
nature of the riot is still not clear; it was over in an hour, and it had no
anti-American aspects. If the United States now sent a naval vessel to Havana,
it might be buying trouble with Spain. Yet if a riot did break out and Americans
were killed, the Administration would be stoned for not having a ship there
to protect them. For several days McKinley wavered; then he ordered the
Maine to Havana, but with the explanation that this was a courtesy visit
demonstrating that so nonsensical were the rumors of danger to American
citizens that our ships could again resume their visits to the island.

As the *Maine* lay at anchor in Havana Harbor, the rebels, with a perfect
sense of timing, released a new propaganda bombshell. In December, 1897,
in a private letter, Señor Enrique Dupuy de Lôme, the Spanish minister at
Washington, had set down his opinions of President McKinley's annual message
to Congress: "Besides the ingrained and inevitable bluntness (*grosería*) with
which it repeated all that the press and public opinion in Spain have said
about Weyler," De Lôme wrote, "it once more shows what McKinley is, weak
and a bidder for the admiration of the crowd, besides being a would-be
politician (*politicastro*) who tries to leave a door open behind himself while
keeping on good terms with the jingoes of his party." De Lôme added: "It

would be very advantageous to take up, even if only for effect, the question of commercial relations, and to have a man of some prominence sent here in order that I may make use of him to carry on a propaganda among the Senators and others in opposition to the junta."

De Lôme had, to be sure, written all this in a private letter (which was stolen by an insurgent spy in the Havana post office), not in his official capacity, and his characterization of McKinley was not wholly without merit, but it was a blunder of the highest magnitude. Not only had De Lôme attacked the President, but he had gone on to suggest that the negotiations then going on over a commercial treaty were not being conducted in good faith. Throughout the letter ran precisely the tone which Hearst had been arguing expressed the Spanish temper—a cold, arrogant contempt for democratic institutions. The State Department immediately cabled Woodford to demand the recall of the Spanish minister, but Madrid had the good fortune of being able to tell Woodford that De Lôme, informed of the disaster the night before, had already resigned.

A week after the publication of the De Lôme indiscretion, at 9:40 on the night of February 15, 1898, came the terrible blow which ended all real hope for peace. In the harbor of Havana, the *Maine* was blown up by an explosion of unknown origin. In an instant, the ship was filled with the sounds of shrieking men and rushing water. The blast occurred in the forward part of the ship where, a half hour before, most of the men had turned in for the night; they were killed in their hammocks. Of the 350 officers and men on board, 260 were killed. By morning the proud *Maine* had sunk into the mud of Havana Harbor.

"Public opinion should be suspended until further report," Captain Sigsbee cabled to Washington, but even Sigsbee could not down his suspicions. The *Maine* had gone to a Spanish possession on a courtesy call, and the *Maine* now lay at the bottom of Havana Harbor. What could it mean but war? "I would give anything if President McKinley would order the fleet to Havana tomorrow," wrote Theodore Roosevelt. "The *Maine* was sunk by an act of dirty treachery on the part of the Spaniards." Volunteers lined up for war service, even though there was no one to enlist them; in New York 500 sharpshooting Westchester businessmen volunteered as a unit for the colors. The *Journal* reported: "The Whole Country Thrills With War Fever."

The cause of the explosion of the *Maine* has never been finally established. That Spain deliberately decided to blow up the *Maine* is inconceivable, although it is possible that it might have been the work of unauthorized Spanish extremists. The one group which had everything to gain from such an episode was the rebels; yet it seems unlikely that either they or Spanish hotheads could have carried out such an act and remained undetected. The most likely explanation is that it was caused by an explosion of internal origin; yet the evidence for this is not conclusive. In any event, this was the explanation that the Navy in 1898 was least willing to consider since it would reflect seriously on the care with which the Navy was operating the *Maine*.

The move toward war seemed relentless. On March 9 Congress unanimously voted $50,000,000 for war preparations. Yet the days went by and there was no war, in part because important sectors of American opinion viewed Hearst's

stories of the atrocious conditions on the island with profound skepticism.
Senator Redfield Proctor of Vermont decided to launch his own investigation
into conditions on the island. On March 17, after a tour of Cuba, Proctor
made one of the most influential speeches in the history of the United States
Senate.

Proctor, who Roosevelt reported was "very ardent for the war," had not
generally been regarded as a jingo, and no man in the Senate commanded greater
respect for personal integrity. Proctor declared that he had gone to Cuba skeptical
of reports of suffering there, and he had come back convinced. "Torn from
their homes, with foul earth, foul air, foul water, and foul food or none, what
wonder that one-half have died and that one-quarter of the living are so
diseased that they can not be saved?" Proctor asked. "Little children are still
walking about with arms and chest terribly emaciated, eyes swollen, and abdomen
bloated to three times the natural size. . . . I was told by one of our consuls that
they have been found dead about the markets in the morning, where they had
crawled, hoping to get some stray bits of food from the early hucksters."

The question of peace or war now lay with McKinley. The Spaniards,
Woodford had conceded, had gone about as far as they could go; but with
the *Maine* in the mud of Havana Harbor, with the country, following Proctor's
speech, crying for war, how much longer could McKinley hold out? The jingoes
were treating his attempt to preserve peace with outright contempt; McKinley,
Roosevelt told his friends, "has no more backbone than a chocolate éclair."

"We will have this war for the freedom of Cuba," Roosevelt shouted at a
Gridiron Dinner on March 26, shaking his fist at Senator Hanna, "in spite of
the timidity of the commercial interests." Nor was McKinley permitted to forget
the political consequences. The Chicago *Times-Herald* warned: "Intervention
in Cuba, peacefully if we can, forcibly if we must, is immediately inevitable.
Our own internal political conditions will not permit its postponement. . . . Let
President McKinley hesitate to rise to the just expectations of the American
people, and who can doubt that 'war for Cuban liberty' will be the crown
of thorns the free silver Democrats and Populists will adopt at the elections this
fall?"

On March 28 the President released the report of the naval court of inquiry
on the *Maine* disaster. "In the opinion of the court the *Maine* was destroyed by
the explosion of a submarine mine, which caused the partial explosion of two or
more of the forward magazines," the report concluded. Although no one was
singled out for blame, the conclusion was inescapable that if Spain had not
willfully done it, Spain had failed to provide proper protection to a friendly
vessel on a courtesy visit in its waters. Overnight a slogan with the ring of a
child's street chant caught the fancy of the country:

Remember the Maine!
To hell with Spain!

"I have no more doubt than that I am now standing in the Senate of the
United States," declared Henry Cabot Lodge, "that that ship was blown up by
a government mine, fired by, or with the connivance of, Spanish officials."

Desiring peace yet afraid of its consequences, McKinley embarked on a policy of attempting to gain the fruits of war without fighting. On March 29 Woodford demanded that Spain agree to an immediate armistice, revoke the reconcentration order, and co-operate with the United States to provide relief; Spain was given 48 hours to reply. On March 31 Spain replied that it had finally revoked the reconcentration orders in the western provinces; that it had made available a credit of three million pesetas to resettle the natives; that it was willing to submit the *Maine* controversy to arbitration; and that it would grant a truce if the insurgents would ask for it. In short, Spain would yield everything we demanded, except that it would not concede defeat; the appeal for a truce would have to come from the rebels. Since the rebels would not make such an appeal, since they were confident of ultimate American intervention, the situation was hopeless; yet Spain had come a long way. Woodford cabled to Washington: "The ministry have gone as far as they dare go to-day. . . . No Spanish ministry would have dared to do one month ago what this ministry has proposed to-day."

For a week the Spaniards attempted to cling to their last shreds of dignity. On Saturday, April 9, Madrid surrendered. Driven to the wall by the American demands, the Spanish foreign minister informed Woodford that the government had decided to grant an armistice in Cuba immediately. Gratified at achieving the final concession, Woodford cabled McKinley: "I hope that nothing will now be done to humiliate Spain, as I am satisfied that the present Government is going, and is loyally ready to go, as fast and as far as it can."

It was too late. McKinley had decided on war. Spain had conceded everything, but Spain had waited too long. Up until the very last moment, Spanish officials had feared that if they yielded to American demands in Cuba, it might mean the overturn of the dynasty, and they preferred even a disastrous war to that. Proud but helpless in the face of American might, many Spanish officials appeared to prefer the dignity of being driven from the island in a heroic defensive war to meek surrender to an American ultimatum. In the end they surrendered and promised reforms. But they had promised reforms before—after the Ten Years' War which ended in 1878—and they had not kept these promises. Throughout the nineteenth century, constitutions had been made and remade, but nothing had changed. Even in the last hours of negotiations with the American minister, they had told Woodford that the President had asked the Pope to intervene, when the President had done nothing of the sort. Even if their intentions were of the best, could they carry them out? Spain had had three full years to end the war in Cuba and, with vastly superior numbers of troops, had not been able to do it. And the insurgents would accept nothing from Madrid, not even peace.

On Monday, April 11, McKinley sent his message to Congress, declaring that "the forcible intervention of the United States as a neutral to stop the war, according to the large dictates of humanity and following many historical precedents" was "justifiable on rational grounds." The fact that Spain had met everything we had asked was buried in two paragraphs of a long plea for war. It took Congress a full week to act. On Monday night, April 18, while the resolution shuttled back and forth between the two chambers and the conference room, congressmen sang "The Battle Hymn of the Republic" and "Dixie" and shook the chamber with the refrain of "Hang General Weyler to a Sour Apple Tree." At three o'clock the next morning the two houses reached an agreement—the United States recognized the independence of Cuba, asserted that we would not acquire Cuba for ourselves, and issued an ultimatum to Spain to withdraw within three days. On April 20 President McKinley signed the resolution. War had come at last. But not quite. Although hostilities had begun, not until four days later did Congress declare war. When it did declare war, it dated it from McKinley's action in establishing a blockade four days before. To the very end, we protested our peaceful intentions as we stumbled headlong into war.

We entered a war in which no vital American interest was involved, and without any concept of its consequences. Although McKinley declared that to enter such a war for high purposes, and then annex territory, would be "criminal aggression," we acquired as a result of the war the Philippines and other parts of an overseas empire we had not intended to get and had no idea how to defend. Although we roundly attacked Spain for not recognizing the rebel government, we, in our turn, refused to recognize the rebels. Although we were shocked by Weyler's policies in Cuba, we were soon in the unhappy position of using savage methods to put down a rebel uprising in the Philippines, employing violence in a measure that easily matched what Weyler had done.

It would be easy to condemn McKinley for not holding out against war, but McKinley showed considerable courage in bucking the tide. McKinley's personal sympathy for the Cubans was sincere; only after his death was it revealed that he had contributed $5,000 anonymously for Cuban relief. It would be even easier to blame it all on Hearst; yet no newspaper can arouse a people that is not willing to be aroused. At root lay the American gullibility about foreign affairs, with the penchant for viewing politics in terms of a simple morality play; equally important were the contempt of the American people for Spain as a cruel but weak Latin nation and the desire for war and expansion which permeated the decade. The American people were not led into war; they got the war they wanted. "I think," observed Senator J. C. Spooner, "possibly the President could have worked out the business without war, but the current was too strong, the demagogues too numerous, the fall elections too near."

three
the depression and psychic crisis

RICHARD HOFSTADTER

*Historians have tended to stress the rational in American
history, that is, to follow choices through a decision-making
process that has consciously weighed alternatives and
rationally selected a course. But Richard Hofstadter
(1916–1970), for over twenty years a teacher of American
intellectual and political history at Columbia University,
devoted a large part of his scholarship to the irrational
behavior of Americans. The following essay, drawn
from* The Paranoid Style in American Politics *(1965), finds
a national psychic crisis leading to imperialism in the
1890s. Hofstadter admitted that his assumptions were
speculative and that psychological research on the past is
difficult. Yet his work has added another dimension to the
study of imperialism and to an explanation of why in
the 1890s, in particular, Americans collected foreign real
estate. Hofstadter's other books include* American Political
Tradition *(1948),* Social Darwinism in American Thought
*(1944, 1955), which carries an interesting chapter on racism
and imperialism,* The Age of Reform *(1955), and* Anti-
Intellectualism in American Life *(1962). The last two
books won Pulitzer Prizes.*

The taking of the Philippine Islands from Spain in 1899
marked a major historical departure for the American
people, a breach in their traditions and a shock to their
established values. To be sure, from their national
beginnings they had constantly engaged in expansion, but
almost entirely into contiguous territory. Now they were

Source: Richard Hofstadter, *The Paranoid Style in American Politics
and Other Essays* (New York: Alfred A. Knopf, 1967), pp.
147–51, 183–86. Copyright © 1952 by Richard Hofstadter.
Reprinted by permission of Alfred A. Knopf, Inc.

extending themselves to distant extra-hemispheric colonies. They were
abandoning a strategy of defense hitherto limited to the continent and its
appurtenances, in favor of a major strategic commitment in the Far East. Thus
far their expansion had been confined to the spread of a relatively homogeneous
population into territories planned from the beginning to develop
self-government; now control was to be imposed by force on millions of ethnic
aliens. The acquisition of the islands, therefore, was understood by
contemporaries on both sides of the debate, as it is readily understood today,
to be a turning point in our history.

To discuss the debate in isolation from other events, however, would be to
deprive it of its full significance. America's entrance into the Philippine
Islands was a by-product of the Spanish-American War. The Philippine crisis
is inseparable from the war crisis, and the war crisis itself is inseparable from a
larger constellation that might be called "the psychic crisis of the 1890's."

Central in the background of the psychic crisis was the great depression
that broke in 1893 and was still very acute when the agitation over the war in
Cuba began. Severe depression, by itself, does not always generate an
emotional crisis as intense as that of the nineties. In the 1870's the country
had been swept by a depression of comparable acuteness and duration which,
however, did not give rise to all the phenomena that appeared in the 1890's
or to very many of them with comparable intensity and impact. It is often said
that the 1890's, unlike the 1870's, form a "watershed" in American history.
The difference between the emotional and intellectual impact of these two
depressions can be measured, I believe, not by the difference in severity, but
rather by reference to a number of singular events that in the 1890's converged
with the depression to heighten its impact upon the public mind.

First in importance was the Populist movement, the free-silver agitation,
the heated campaign of 1896. For the first time in our history a depression had
created a protest movement strong enough to capture a major party and raise the
specter, however unreal, of drastic social convulsion. Second was the maturation
and bureaucratization of American business, the completion of its essential
industrial plant, and the development of trusts on a scale sufficient to stir
the anxiety that the old order of competitive opportunities was approaching
an eclipse. Third, and of immense symbolic importance, was the apparent
filling up of the continent and the disappearance of the frontier line. We now
know how much land had not yet been taken up and how great were the
remaining possibilities for internal expansion both in business and on the land;
but to the mind of the 1890's it seemed that the resource that had engaged
the energies of the people for three centuries had been used up. The
frightening possibility suggested itself that a serious juncture in the nation's
history had come. As Frederick Jackson Turner expressed it in his famous
paper of 1893: "Now, four centuries from the discovery of America, at the
end of one hundred years of life under the Constitution, the frontier has gone,
and with its going has closed the first period of American history."

To middle-class citizens who had been brought up to think in terms of the
nineteenth-century order, the outlook seemed grim. Farmers in the staple-growing
region had gone mad over silver and Bryan; workers were stirring in bloody

struggles like the Homestead and Pullman strikes; the supply of new land seemed at an end; the trust threatened the spirit of business enterprise; civic corruption was at a high point in the large cities; great waves of seemingly unassimilable immigrants arrived yearly and settled in hideous slums. To many historically conscious writers, the nation appeared overripe, like an empire ready for collapse through a stroke from outside or through internal upheaval. Acute as the situation was for all those who lived by the symbols of national power—for the governing and thinking classes—it was especially poignant for young people, who would have to make their careers in the dark world that seemed to be emerging.

The symptomatology of the crisis would record several tendencies in popular thought and behavior that had previously existed only in pale and tenuous form. These symptoms were manifest in two quite different moods. The key to one of them was an intensification of protest and humanitarian reform. Populism, utopianism, the rise of the Christian Social gospel, the growing intellectual interest in socialism, the social settlement movement that appealed so strongly to the college generation of the nineties, the quickening of protest and social criticism in the realistic novel—all these are expressions of this mood. The other mood was one of national self-assertion, aggression, expansion. The motif of the first was social sympathy; of the second, national power. During the 1890's far more patriotic groups were founded than in any other decade of our history; the naval theories of Captain Mahan were gaining in influence; naval construction was booming; there was an immense quickening of the American cult of Napoleon and a vogue of the virile and martial writings of Rudyard Kipling; young Theodore Roosevelt became the exemplar of the vigorous, masterful, out-of-doors man; the revival of European imperialism stirred speculation over what America's place would be in the world of renewed colonial rivalries, and in some stirred a demand to get into the imperial race to avoid the risk of being overwhelmed by other powers. But most significant was the rising tide of jingoism, a matter of constant comment among observers of American life during the decade.

Jingoism, of course, was not new in American history. But during the 1870's and 1880's the American public had been notably quiescent about foreign relations. There had been expansionist statesmen, but they had been blocked by popular apathy, and our statecraft had been restrained. Grant had failed dismally in his attempt to acquire Santo Domingo; our policy toward troubled Hawaii had been cautious; in 1877 an offer of two Haitian naval harbors had been spurned. In responding to Haiti, Secretary of State Frelinghuysen had remarked that "the policy of this Government . . . has tended toward avoidance of possessions disconnected from the main continent." Henry Cabot Lodge, in his life of George Washington published in 1889, observed that foreign relations then filled "but a slight place in American politics, and excite generally only a languid interest." Within a few years this comment would have seemed absurd. In 1895, Russell A. Alger reported to Lodge, after reading one of Lodge's own articles to a Cincinnati audience, that he was convinced by the response that foreign policy, "more than anything else, touches the public pulse of today." The history of the 1890's is the history of public agitation over expansionist issues and of quarrels with other nations. . . .

Since Julius W. Pratt published his *Expansionists of 1898* in 1936, it has been obvious that any interpretation of America's entry upon the paths of imperialism in the nineties in terms of rational economic motives would not fit the facts, and that a historian who approached the event with preconceptions no more supple than those, say, of Lenin's *Imperialism* would be helpless. This is not to say that markets and investments have no bearing; they do, but there are features of the situation that they do not explain at all. Insofar as the economic factor was important, it can be better studied by looking at the relation between the depression, the public mood, and the political system.

The alternative explanation has been the equally simple idea that the war was a newspapers' war. This notion, once again, has some point, but it certainly does not explain the war itself, much less its expansionist result. The New Deal period, when the political successes of F.D.R. were won in the face of overwhelming newspaper opposition, showed that the press is not powerful enough to impose upon the public mind a totally uncongenial view of public events. It must operate roughly within the framework of public predispositions. Moreover, not all the papers of the nineties were yellow journals. We must inquire into the structure of journalistic power and also into the views of the owners and editors to find out what differentiated the sensational editors and publishers from those of the conservative press.

There is still another qualification that must be placed upon the role of the press: the press itself, whatever it can do with opinion, does not have the power to precipitate opinion into action. That is something that takes place within the *political* process, and we cannot tell that part of the story without examining the state of party rivalries, the origin and goals of the political elites, and indeed the entire political context. We must, then, supplement our story about the role of the newspapers with at least two other factors: the state of the public temper upon which the newspapers worked, and the manner in which party rivalries deflected domestic clashes into foreign aggression. Here a perennial problem of politics under the competitive two-party system became manifest again in the 1890's. When there is, for whatever reason, a strong current of jingoism running in the channels of public sentiment, party competition tends to speed it along. If the party in power is behaving circumspectly, the opposition tends to beat the drums. For example, in 1896, with Cleveland still in office, the Republican platform was much more exigent on the Cuba issue. When McKinley came into office and began to show reluctance to push toward intervention, the Democratic party became a center of interventionist pressure; this pressure was promptly supplemented by a large number of Republicans who, quite aside from their agreement on the issue, were concerned about its effect on the fate of their party.

When we examine the public temper, we find that the depression, together with such other events as the approaching completion of the settlement of the continent, the growth of trusts, and the intensification of internal social conflict, had brought to large numbers of people intense frustrations in their economic lives and their careers. To others they had brought anxiety that a period of stagnation in national wealth and power had set in. The restlessness of the discontented classes had been heightened by the defeat of Bryan in 1896. The anxieties about the nation's position had been increased among statesmen and publicists by the revival of world imperialism, in particular by the feeling that America was threatened by Germany, Russia, and Japan. The expansionist statesmen themselves were drawn largely from a restless upper-middle-class elite that had been fighting an unrewarding battle for conservative reform in domestic politics and looked with some eagerness toward a more spacious field of action.

Men often respond to frustration with acts of aggression, and allay their anxieties by threatening acts against others. It is revealing that the underdog forces in American society showed a considerably higher responsiveness to the idea of war with Spain than the groups that were satisfied with their economic or political positions. Our entry into the Philippines then aroused the interest of conservative groups that had been indifferent to the quixotism of freeing Cuba but were alert to the possibility of capturing new markets. Imperialism appealed to members of both the business and the political elites as an enlargement of the sphere of American power and profits; many of the underdogs also responded to this new note of national self-assertion.

* * *

Clearly this attempt to see the war and expansion in the light of social history has led us onto the high and dangerous ground of social psychology and into the arena of conjecture. But simple rationalistic explanations of national behavior will also leave us dissatisfied. What I have attempted here is merely a preliminary sketch of a possible explanatory model. Further inquiry might make it seem more plausible at some points, more questionable at others.

four
theodore roosevelt and his imperialist friends

HOWARD K. BEALE

*Howard K. Beale (1899–1959), for many years a professor
of history at the University of Wisconsin, was invited in
the mid-1950s to deliver the Albert Shaw lectures at
Johns Hopkins University. From these lectures grew*
Theodore Roosevelt and the Rise of America to World
Power *(1956), a lengthy, widely researched study that found
Roosevelt and a small clique of imperialist friends
responsible for the major decisions of American foreign
policy at the turn of the century. When he prepared his
lectures and book, Beale was dismayed by the "present state
of international relations that threatens to destroy
civilization itself," and he sought to explain the roots
of America's Cold War foreign policy. He found a certain
inexorability to American foreign relations since Roosevelt's
days, and he believed Roosevelt shaped it. Beale asks us
to consider whether certain individuals, public opinion,
or "blind forces" determine history.*

Alone Roosevelt could have accomplished little. But, as a
member of a group of men strategically placed to make
themselves felt, he became a leader of the movement to win

Source: Howard K. Beale, *Theodore Roosevelt and the Rise of
America to World Power* (Baltimore: The Johns Hopkins Press,
1956), pp. 20–41, 54–63. Copyright © 1956 by Johns Hopkins
Press. Used by permission of the publisher.

for America her place in the world. Among these articulate men Henry Cabot
Lodge, with a new Ph.D., had been a young instructor at Harvard when
Theodore was an undergraduate, but they had become friends only in the
presidential campaign of 1884. By 1889 Lodge had gone to Congress and
Roosevelt was Civil Service Commissioner. Henry Adams, whom Roosevelt
knew at Harvard, had now built a house in Lafayette Square where Roosevelt
and his friends dropped in to run the world over cups of Adams tea.
Henry's brother Brooks came often to Washington and moved in the Roosevelt-
Lodge inner circle. In 1889 he had married Nanni Lodge's sister. . . .

Among Roosevelt's imperialistic intimates, too, in Washington, was
professional diplomat William W. Rockhill, expert on Far Eastern affairs,
who served as Chief Clerk, Third Assistant, and finally as Assistant Secretary
of State between 1893 and 1897. In Washington Roosevelt came to know
William E. Chandler, who, as Secretary of the Navy under Chester A. Arthur,
had fathered the modern navy and was now old guard senator from New
Hampshire. Another associate was Senator William P. Frye of Maine, who
shared Chandler's views. Among Roosevelt's close friends were Benjamin F.
Tracy, Harrison's Secretary of the Navy, Charles H. Davis, Lodge's
brother-in-law, then commander in the Navy and chief of naval intelligence,
and retired Admiral Stephen B. Luce, a strong supporter of the Mahan point of
view. In 1887, while himself giving a lecture on the War of 1812, Roosevelt
met Alfred T. Mahan at the Naval War College where Mahan was stationed as
instructor. In 1890 and again in 1893 Roosevelt reviewed in the *Atlantic
Monthly,* in 1894 in the *Political Science Quarterly,* and in 1897 in the *New York
Sun* Mahan's books on sea power, which he praised in highest terms. By 1890
Lodge, Roosevelt, and Mahan had begun exchanging views. In 1890 Roosevelt,
Lodge, Luce, and Davis combined to try to save Mahan from assignment to
sea duty so that he could continue full-time his propaganda for expansion. "Oh
what idiots we have had to deal with," Roosevelt exploded to Mahan when
the Navy Department insisted upon sending him to sea.

During the first half of the second Cleveland administration Roosevelt, as
Civil Service Commissioner, stayed on in Washington and was a vigorous
member of a group critical of Cleveland; and, even after he became
Police Commissioner in New York, he kept in touch with Lodge, Rockhill,
Hay, and the Adamses. He corresponded with them, entertained them at dinners
in his sister's home in New York, and saw them on visits to the Lodges in
Washington. Eliminated from the diplomatic service by the Democratic
President, Henry White in 1893 joined the group and his views delighted
Roosevelt. In 1895 Richard Olney became Cleveland's Secretary of State and
Rockhill was promoted to be Assistant Secretary, both of them already adopted
into the Roosevelt circle. "In spite of your Democratic politics," he wrote
Rockhill, "I *have* to be proud of Olney and yourself."

Chandler and Frye, and eventually Lodge and several others of Roosevelt's
friends, were powerful members of the Senate, and Lodge, Mahan, and
Roosevelt reached an élite following with books and essays. Mahan lectured
to naval officers and published articles for the general public and supplied
other jingoes with arguments so phrased as to catch popular attention. Charles

A. Dana of the *New York Sun* was a powerful aid. Two secretaries of State, a secretary of the Navy, an assistant secretary of State, and an assistant secretary of the Navy were strategically placed to help. Collectively these men were a potent influence in giving American participation in world affairs a nationalist and imperialist cast.

What was it that led Roosevelt and his friends to urge an expansionist rôle upon us? A number of fundamental preconceptions can be identified, along with a host of associated ideas. First, the imperialists were strong nationalists and were impelled by national pride. "We're a gr-reat people," said Mr. Dooley with the Roosevelt sort of nationalist in mind. "We ar-re that. An' th' best iv it is, we know we ar-re." Roosevelt was determined that we should put the interests and honor of the United States above those of other nations. He wanted therefore to drive every European power "off this continent." "I am not hostile," he explained, "to any European power in the abstract. I am simply American first and last, and therefore hostile to any power which wrongs us." When his Catholic friend Maria Storer wrote him that the Pope was angry with Archbishop Ireland for not stopping the War with Spain, Roosevelt replied vehemently: "I would resent as an impertinence any European, whether Pope, Kaiser, Czar or President, daring to be angry with an American because of his action or nonaction as regards any question between America and an outside nation. . . . If any man, clerical or lay, Bishop, Archbishop, priest, or civilian, was in any way guilty of treasonable practices with Spain during our war, he should be shot or hung. . . ."

*   *   *

Second, Roosevelt was convinced, as are many nationalists in most countries, that his country would never act unjustly or wrongly. Hence, whatever position America took was right. American expansion became part of a crusade for the right. Consequently, whoever at home or abroad opposed American expansion was morally derelict. In Roosevelt's case this moral purpose was unusually strong. Carl Schurz said: Roosevelt's conviction that the honor of the country demands his continuance in office leads him to twist facts in a manner that we would have to call "disingenuous, did we not think that he believes them to be true." He seems to have the impression, Schurz declared, "that everything apt to promote his chances [of reëlection] is good and every adverse influence wicked, and that, therefore, those who decide to vote against him— about one-half the voters of the United States, more or less—are unpatriotic citizens and bad Americans." Thus his and Lodge's quarrel with political opponents in Massachusetts in 1905 became a matter of ethical principles and anyone that opposed him and Lodge showed "a lack of moral sense." Thus, in his disagreements with the Senate, senators that vigorously opposed him were "demagogues" or "crooks." . . . Similarly, in international affairs he could not imagine a situation where there could be any justification in opposing America. He wished to make America so strong that, whatever she did, no one would dare oppose the "right" by trying to thwart her. "Peace," he said, "comes not to the coward or to the timid, but to him who will do no wrong and is too strong to allow others to wrong him." In short, Roosevelt believed only in "just wars," but any war America fought would be "just." The war with Spain he pronounced "the most absolutely righteous foreign war" of the nineteenth century. So morality, America's idea of international morality, became an important element in the foreign policy of the Roosevelt expansionists. Their effective advocacy greatly strengthened in our diplomacy the force of moral conviction with which many Americans tend to face public issues. They accustomed many admirers to believing American policies always moral and opponents' aims immoral in international affairs, however reprehensible American actions might occasionally seem to non-Americans.

Third, Roosevelt shared with other imperialists a sense of Anglo-Saxon superiority to peoples over whom we were extending our rule and also superiority to some of those with whose imperialism we would compete. Roosevelt's sense of superiority was not the usual sort of racism preached by the more extreme leaders of his own day, still less the brand found on the Pacific Coast of the United States or in the American South, or yet in Nazi Germany. Roosevelt had studied under John W. Burgess at Columbia and this may have introduced him to a belief in the special ability of Anglo-Saxons to rule backward peoples. But his attitudes toward race were not peculiar to Burgess and Columbia; there were many others that believed in Anglo-Saxonism. . . . Actually, to Roosevelt and many of his contemporaries "race" was no more than a loose term for any given group, distinguished by its color, language, degree of industrial development, or national culture, to be used as the situation demanded.

In reviewing Pearson's *National Life and Character* in 1894 he accepted the concept of white superiority and spoke even of the Chinese with their ancient culture as an inferior race. He was concerned about the well-being of the white race. He admitted he had once taken "the educated view of the Chinese question," but he had come to see that the Chinese had to be kept out of America because "his presence would be ruinous to the white race." He came to feel that even the Japanese, whom he admired, could not be admitted to this country. In 1897 he told James Bryce that we ought to take Hawaii "in the interests of the White race." Democracy, he thought, had justified itself by keeping "for the white race the best portions of the new world's surface." . . . At Oxford in 1910 he declared that the period of supremacy of the white race had seen an "unexampled spread of civilized mankind over the world," an "unexampled advance of man's dominion over nature," and "a literary and artistic activity to be matched in but one previous epoch."

Yet he was unlike many racists in that he laid these differences of "race" to acquired characteristics and to the effect of geographic environment. In the common parlance of his day, he talked of Latin Americans contemptuously as Dagoes, but his contempt was not for their Latin origin. It was provoked by the weakness and inability of these particular Latins to rule themselves effectively. Again like most Americans, he felt superior to Filipinos and Chinese. One of his strongest words of contumely was to dub a weak incompetent a Chinese. He talked of the Chinese as a backward race. Yet, though they were of the same color and were ethnically similar to the Chinese, he felt as much admiration for the Japanese who were strong and efficient as he felt contempt for the weakness and inefficiency of the Chinese. Japan, he pointed out, though "in blood and in culture" as "remote as possible" from "our ancestral descent," and though "keeping most of what was strongest in her ancient character and traditions, has assimilated with curious completeness most of the characteristics that have given power and leadership to the West."

* * *

Finally, in Roosevelt's race attitudes there was no element of contempt for an individual member of a race who had attained qualities superior to other members of a backward people. So thoroughly imbued was he with what he considered the American quality of individualism, such respect did he have for the sacredness of the individual personality that he judged separate men as individual human beings, not as members of a class, a race, or a nation. So any particular Negro, Chinese, or Filipino who displayed qualities he admired was to him an admirable person and an equal. When he spoke of national groups, or races, or peoples he spoke in general and classed each as a group in a category superior or inferior to other groups. Individuals, though, he judged as individuals. . . .

This superior civilization that Roosevelt associated with English-speaking people is a little hard to define from his speeches and writings. In it, however, was a strong mixture of manly virtues, of industrial development, of power to defend oneself effectively; in it, too, were an ability to provide orderly government, an inherited set of political institutions superior to those of anyone else, and respect for free individuals, and for the various freedoms won through the centuries by Western Europeans. Roosevelt had studied at Harvard and Columbia in a day when scholars were tracing our institutions back of Magna Carta into the forests of Germany. He always understood how long it had taken to attain the English-speaking civilization and he profoundly respected the heritage. Its preservation and extension was in his mind the greatest attainable good, even if it had to be extended by force.

For "backward people" Theodore Roosevelt had no particular concern when they stood in the way of "civilization." In 1915 he justified his having ignored the wishes of the Colombians, who owned the territory where he wished to build a canal, by explaining that the Colombians were not a superior but an inferior people. Sensitive lest our action toward Colombia be compared in 1915 to Germany's violation of the rights of Belgium, he explained that "the Belgians were as 'superior' as the Germans," whereas "to talk of Colombia as a responsible Power to be dealt with as we would deal with Holland or Belgium or Switzerland or Denmark is a mere absurdity." "The analogy" of Colombians, he insisted, "is with a group of Sicilian or Calabrian bandits. . . . You could no more make an agreement with the Colombian rulers than you could nail currant jelly to the wall." "The Canal," he explained, "was for the benefit of the entire world. Should the blackmailing greed of the Bogotá ring stand in the way of civilization? . . . I determined that I would do what ought to be done without regard to them."

Yet Roosevelt was not unmindful of "backward" peoples when they did not stand in the way of the extension of civilization. Indeed, much of our imperialist activity he justified upon the ground of serving the "backward" peoples. He shared the conviction of many Americans of his day that the superior white man must bear the burden of civilizing colonial peoples of the world, if necessary against the will of those peoples. "A nation's first duty is within its own borders," he conceded, but "it is not thereby absolved from facing its duties in the world as a whole; and if it refuses to do so, it merely forfeits its right to struggle for a place among the peoples that shape the destiny of mankind." It is cowardly for us to shrink from solving the problems of the West Indies and the Philippines, "for solved they must be, if not by us, then by some stronger and more manful race." "It is our duty toward the people living in barbarism to see that they are freed from their chains," he told Minnesotans a fortnight before he became President, "and we can free them only by destroying barbarism itself. . . ."

* * *

Closely tied to his pride in America and his sense of her moral rectitude and her superiority to others was a special brand of national honor. Roosevelt, when his pride was aroused or his will crossed, sometimes just reacted, as many adults do, like a child determined to have his own way and to resort to fisticuffs if thwarted. This tendency developed into a kind of national honor that made one's standing as a strong nation depend upon making other weaker nations understand that they could not defy the wishes of the great power. "Some time soon I shall have to spank some little brigand of a South American republic," he told his brother-in-law in 1905. Our integrity as a world power demanded similarly that we make the Chinese understand by force if necessary not only that they could not stage a Boxer Rebellion and take the lives of foreigners whom they did not wish in their country, but that they could no more be permitted to put pressure on a great power through the legitimate and effective method of boycotting the great power's goods. Roosevelt's definition of national honor not only required that we must prevent the taking of American lives or seizing of American property in a small Latin American country, but that we could not permit the "Dagoes" of Colombia to question our building a canal on our terms where we wanted to build it through their territory. . . .

Actually Roosevelt was confused about the whole problem of war and peace. He and his associates came close to seeking war for its own sake. Ignorant of modern war, Roosevelt romanticized war, and fighting in the Spanish War was not of a sort to dispel the romanticism. Like many young men tamed by civilization into law-abiding but adventureless living, he needed an outlet for the pent-up primordial man in him and found it in fighting and killing, vicariously or directly, in hunting or in war. Indeed he had a thoroughly good time in war when war came. He would have hesitated to proclaim openly that he liked war. Yet there was something dull and effeminate about peace. A civilized tradition drew him back from open advocacy of war. Yet personally he gloried in war, was thrilled by military history, and placed warlike qualities high in his scale of values. Without consciously desiring it, he thought a little war now and then stimulated admirable qualities in men. Certainly preparation for war did.

Though he valued the blessings of peace, he craved the excitements of war. He therefore sought a big navy because it would prevent war, but also because it was such fun to have a big navy. In the sense of power that ordering ships about gave him he found exhilaration and perhaps compensation for unfulfilled yearnings of a sickly boy whose boyish urges had been unsatisfied. Boylike he wanted many contradictory and mutually exclusive satisfactions and the logical qualities of mind necessary to perceive the contradictions in his desires had not been part of his intellectual training. In 1885 a college chum had written, "He would like above all things to go to war with some one. He has just walked out of the hotel with a rifle over his shoulder. . . . He . . . wants to be killing something all the time." "Frankly I don't know that I should be sorry to see a bit of a spar with Germany," he confided to Spring Rice in 1889. "The burning of New York and a few other sea coast cities would be a good object lesson in the need of an adequate system of coast defenses," he explained, "and I think it would have a good effect on our large German population to force them to an ostentatiously patriotic display of anger against Germany." . . . Again, "It is very difficult for me not to wish a war with Spain, for such a war would result at once in getting a proper Navy." In 1897 he declared, "In strict confidence, . . . I should welcome almost any war, for I think this country needs one." He "gushes over war," protested William James, "as the ideal condition of human society, for the manly strenuousness which it involves, and treats peace as a condition of blubberlike and swollen ignobility, fit only for huckstering weaklings, dwelling in gray twilight and heedless of the higher life. . . . One foe is as good as another, for aught he tells us."

The Roosevelt-Lodge expansionists who took the American people into an imperialist struggle for world power were not primarily concerned with American economic interests around the world. Nor did they attempt to justify expansion chiefly on economic grounds. Where they were interested in economic matters it was because economic advantages won converts to imperialist policies or enhanced the prestige of the country. Economic factors *were* important in imperialism and were to become important in American expansionist foreign policy of the twentieth century. But the primary concern of Roosevelt and his fellow-expansionists was power and prestige and the naval strength that would bring power and prestige. They gloried in the thought of American greatness and power that their expansionist policies would create. "I wish to see the United States the dominant power on the Pacific Ocean," Roosevelt wrote in 1900. "Our people are neither cravens nor weaklings and we face the future high of heart and confident of soul eager to do the great work of a great world power."

* * *

For the moment or for the long run Roosevelt, Lodge, Mahan, and their friends considered overseas empire the climax of their program. Cuba they at first hoped to win without fighting if we could become so strong that Spain would not dare object to our encouraging revolution in the Spanish islands. They also

wanted Puerto Rico. Roosevelt, along with Lodge and White, tried to get the
government to acquire the Danish West Indies. "I believe we should build
the Nicaraguan canal at once," he wrote Mahan in May, 1897. He even hoped
to take Canada or at least to force Britain to relinquish control of it. He
criticized Cleveland for not seizing it. Farther afield he wanted Hawaii and
Samoa. When the Philippines entered his dreams is not clear.

* * *

Thus by the time the anti-imperialist Cleveland left office, and two years before
the Spanish War awoke most Americans to our new rôle, Roosevelt, Lodge, and
their coterie had formulated an imperialist philosophy for America, had mapped
out a program, and had marshaled their forces. America had with their hearty
support successfully stood up as a great power to a great power at risk of
war. The stage was set to win us a place in the sun of world power, if the jingoes
could ever win control of the government.

Republican victory gave this group of strategically placed expansionists their
chance in 1897 to apply the principles they had long espoused. A few men in
powerful positions were able to plunge the nation into an imperialist career
that it never explicitly decided to follow. Each worked to promote the other for
high position. Lodge promoted John Hay for the secretaryship of State. He
journeyed besides to Canton, Ohio, to appeal personally to President-elect
McKinley for Henry White's appointment as secretary of Legation in London
and for Roosevelt's as assistant secretary of the Navy. "I am afraid he is too
pugnacious. . . . I want peace and I am told that your friend Theodore is
always getting into rows with everybody," McKinley protested to Maria Storer.
"Give him a chance," Mrs. Storer pleaded, "to prove that he can be peaceful."
Judge William H. Taft, a new member of the group, pleaded Roosevelt's
cause with McKinley. "The truth is, Will, Roosevelt is always in such a state
of mind," McKinley told Taft. But Roosevelt was appointed Assistant Secretary
of the Navy; White went to London as Secretary, and Hay as Ambassador. . . .

Lodge, Roosevelt, and Mahan, in constant consultation, worked on
Secretary of State Sherman and President McKinley to get them to seize Hawaii,
and Roosevelt prepared a memorandum for Long to use in Cabinet meeting.
"If only we had some good man in the place of John Sherman as Secretary
of State there would not be a hitch," Roosevelt wrote Mahan. "Do nothing
unrighteous; but as regards the [political] problem [involved in annexation],
take the islands first," Mahan prodded Roosevelt in May, 1897, "and solve
afterwards." Finally, Lodge, Roosevelt, Assistant Secretary of State William R.
Day, and others persuaded McKinley over Sherman's head. On June 16 an
annexation treaty was signed. Sherman himself, ignorant of the treaty
negotiations, had assured the Japanese minister that no treaty was
being negotiated, and so when the treaty was announced Japan protested.
Roosevelt answered Japan's protest in a speech in which he declared: "The
United States is not in a position which requires her to ask Japan or any other
foreign Power what territory it shall or shall not acquire." Even the Republican
New York Tribune suggested that he "leave to the Department of State the

declaration of . . . foreign policy," which "is not the business of the Assistant
Secretary of the Navy." Long reprimanded him severely for this speech,
but Lodge felt: "You were all right in what you said." So too, to Roosevelt's
surprise, did McKinley, who thought "it was only the headlines that were
wrong." Roosevelt wrote an article in *Gunton's Magazine* pleading for
ratification. He, Lodge, and others made speeches and worked on doubtful
senators. Roosevelt, Lodge, Mahan, and White were "sick" when they thought
how easily the Harrison Treaty could have been ratified in 1893. On
March 17 the Treaty was laid finally aside and the annexationists won Hawaii
only in 1898 and then by joint resolution. By that time, however, Roosevelt was
busy fighting a war against Spain.

Hawaii seemed important to Mahan, Lodge, and Roosevelt for several
reasons. Commercially Hawaii was necessary to insure us "a share in the vast
trade and commerce of the Pacific." Second, "The people . . . who have
civilized and developed those islands are Americans. . . . We have not . . .
any right to leave them to be engulfed by an Asiatic immigration," Lodge
contended. Ignoring the presence of more Orientals than whites, Lodge argued
on democratic grounds that "a majority of whites and natives, who alone have a
right to speak, seek annexation." Similarly disregarding the huge Oriental
population Roosevelt pronounced the native Hawaiians unable to govern, and
the whites therefore entitled to rule the islands. Besides, if we did not take
Hawaii, Japan, Germany, or Britain would. Annexation would advance
civilization, said Roosevelt, and taking the islands was the only policy
compatible with our interests. "We did not create the Hawaiian Islands,"
Roosevelt told New York Republicans in February, 1898; "they already exist.
We merely have to face the alternative of taking them ourselves and making
them the outpost for the protection of the Pacific Coast or else of seeing them
taken by any powerful nation with which we are at war, and at once
transformed into the most dangerous possible base of operations against our
Pacific cities. We cannot help Hawaii's being either a strong defense to us or a
perpetual menace. We can only decide whether we will now take the islands
when offered to us as a gift, or by force try to conquer them from the first
powerful nation with which we may become embroiled."

Our interest in Samoa was chiefly strategic. At the time we acquired
American Samoa, Secretary of State Hay wrote, "Our interests in the Archipelago
were very meagre, always excepting our interest in Pago Pago, which was of
the most vital importance. It is the finest harbor in the Pacific and absolutely
indispensable to us."

Roosevelt originally wanted to drive Spain out of Cuba by a show of force
short of war. In 1895 Lodge conferred with Prime Minister Antonio Cánovas
del Castillo of Spain about Cuba. Throughout 1896 Lodge and Roosevelt
sought intervention, not to annex Cuba, but to win her independence. In close
accord with Theodore in these matters Lodge conferred in 1896 with the
Committee of Cuban Patriots; he served on the Senate sub-committee on
Cuba; he went to see Cleveland to urge him to act; he supported Senate
resolutions in favor of Cuban independence; he formulated a principle on
intervention in Cuba strikingly similar to Roosevelt's later corollary to the

Monroe Doctrine. In regard to Cuba as in regard to Venezuela, business men protested over the risk of war involved in these policies.

As Assistant Secretary of the Navy Roosevelt had given up action short of war and was doing all in his power to promote war with Spain over Cuba. "I am a quietly rampant 'Cuba Libre' man," Roosevelt wrote his sister in January, 1897. He invited key senators to the Metropolitan Club with a special envoy just back from Cuba. By March, 1898, he was writing Mahan, "I can hardly see how we can avoid intervening in Cuba if we are to retain our self-respect as a nation."

* * *

Since he could not persuade the Administration of which he was part to go to war, the best Roosevelt could do was to prepare the Navy for war in case McKinley changed his mind. "If we drift into the war butt end foremost, and go at it higgledy-piggledy fashion," he protested, "we shall meet with occasional difficulties." But he was determined that all the preparations in his power should be made to reduce those difficulties to a minimum. He tried to keep naval vessels in good condition and so disposed as to be most useful if war came. He opposed laying up vessels. Orders were issued that concentrated our ships. He hoped to manoeuver a head-on sea fight and urged his German friend Speck to come to observe "the pretty fight" it would be. He discussed war plans with naval officers, tried to prevent taking ships out of service, and even sought to buy more. When on February 25, 1898, Secretary Long went home early intending to take a day's rest and Roosevelt became Acting Secretary for three or four hours, he made the most of his opportunity. He sent a momentous cable to George Dewey. He issued instructions to the European and South Atlantic squadrons where to rendezvous, if war broke out. He ordered commanders all over the world to keep their ships filled with the best possible coal. He bought all the coal he could buy in the Far East. He sent a "strictly confidential" letter to the New York adjutant general urging him to make plans for supplying men in case of war. In short, Long found next morning that Roosevelt "in his precipitate way" had "come very near causing more of an explosion than happened to the *Maine*." In his diary Long described those few hours: "He immediately began to launch peremptory orders: distributing ships; ordering ammunition, which there is no means to move, to places where there is no means to store it; sending for Captain Barker to come on about the guns of the Vesuvius . . . , sending messages to Congress for immediate legislation, authorizing the enlistment of an unlimited number of seamen; and ordering guns from the Navy Yard at Washington to New York." Indeed, Long recorded, "He has gone at things like a bull in a china shop." Long abandoned his day's vacation and returned to the office early next morning and never left Roosevelt in charge again even for part of a day. Long, Speaker Reed, Chairman Charles A. Boutelle and Eugene Hale of the naval committees of Congress were distressed by Roosevelt's precipitateness. Long concluded that the serious illness of Mrs. Roosevelt and young Ted had "accentuated . . . his natural nervousness" so much that he was "hardly fit to be entrusted with the responsibility of the Department at this critical time."

Long's error lay in ascribing Roosevelt's action to impulsiveness. The orders were deliberate acts that Roosevelt and his friends had discussed for months but had been unable to accomplish. Long's absence gave Roosevelt the chance to carry out carefully-laid and well-matured plans to prepare better for war than he had been able to persuade his associates to do when he was not in command.

Apparently the concurrently developing problem of the Philippines was not part of a well-thought-out Far Eastern policy. None of the expansionists seems to have coveted the islands until Mahan found need for them as he planned naval strategy of the hoped-for war with Spain. Then in September, 1897, Roosevelt wrote Lodge, "Our Asiatic squadron should blockade, and if possible take, Manilla [*sic*]." From then on Roosevelt worked to have the Asiatic squadron in shape for that purpose, and in March he persuaded Long to order the *Baltimore* to Asia. When a commander was needed for the Asiatic squadron, Roosevelt, with his eye on war and the Philippines, was determined to have a fighting man who would act with daring. Over the heads of senior officers and against political opposition Roosevelt manoeuvered Dewey's appointment. When Dewey found insufficient coal and could not get any through normal channels, Roosevelt cut through red tape and navy routine and had coal sent him. Then among his momentous activities of February 25 Roosevelt cabled Dewey instructions of far-reaching consequences: "Order the squadron except *Monocacy* to Hong Kong. Keep full of coal. In the event of declaration war Spain, your duty will be to see that the Spanish squadron does not leave the Asiatic coast, and then offensive operations in Philippine Islands." Dewey's talks with Roosevelt in Washington had made it clear what Roosevelt wanted. Now he had authorization. Long was upset, but as Lodge put it, "The deed was done. The wise word of readiness had been spoken and was not recalled." The Assistant Secretary had seized the opportunity given by Long's absence to insure our grabbing the Philippines without a decision to do so by either Congress or the President, or least of all the people. Thus was important history made not by economic forces or democratic decisions but through the grasping of chance authority by a man with daring and a program.

five
the courageous leadership of president william mckinley

JOHN A. S. GRENVILLE AND GEORGE B. YOUNG

*The coauthors of the following essay dissent vigorously from
the conclusions of Leuchtenburg and Beale. They insist
that neither public opinion nor an imperialist clique took
America to war, but rather an astute and courageous
president who acted in the national interest. John A. S.
Grenville (b. 1928) and George B. Young (b. 1913)
collaborated on* Politics, Strategy, and American Diplomacy
*(1966), which concludes that American foreign policy
—imperialism—was wise. Grenville, who teaches at the
University of Birmingham, England, has also written*
Lord Salisbury and Foreign Policy *(1964). Young has
enjoyed a successful career in business and law in Chicago
since receiving his doctorate in history from Yale
University in 1939.*

William McKinley is considered to be something less than a
great president. "There are traces of virtue, but few of
character," is one recent verdict. Theodore Roosevelt
thought: "The President only loves one thing in the whole
world and that is his wife. He treats everyone with equal
favor; their worth to him is solely dependent on the

Source: John A. S. Grenville and George B. Young, *Politics,
Strategy, and American Diplomacy: Studies in Foreign Policy,
1873–1917* (New Haven, Conn.: Yale University Press, 1966),
pp. 239–46, 251–52, 256–66, 286. Copyright © 1966 by
Yale University. Reprinted by permission of the publisher.

advantages he could derive from them . . . he keeps his ear to the ground, listens and then follows public opinion." McKinley baffled him. The President was not a leader of men in the sense Roosevelt aspired to be. His conduct on the eve of the war with Spain was pusillanimous—so runs the general consensus of opinion. He allowed the jingoes to drive him into war; he lacked the strength and courage Cleveland had shown in a similar situation when he paid public pressure no heed. But these are not altogether sound judgments.

The price of dynamic presidential leadership too often proves to be a barren legislative record; Congress is suspicious of executive power. McKinley did not complain of the conduct of Congress; he was after all an adroit politician who had seen long service in the Capitol. He accepted the right of Congress to a voice in foreign affairs philosophically; the reaction of Congress was an important consideration in the formation of his policy. "We cannot always do what is best," he remarked to one congressman, "but we can do what is practical at the time." In deciding policy the President is not a free agent. Some Presidents have bypassed Congress and appealed to the people for support; they have more often than not seen their policies fail. McKinley chose the opposite course of attempting to manage Congress by skillful maneuvering.

Although it seems curious that historians should have perpetuated a picture of McKinley as a man lacking backbone and political courage, there is perhaps one explanation. Much of the historical discussion of this period reflects a feeling of guilt about America's imperialist role in 1898, an assumption that Cleveland represented what was good and resisted what was bad, and that in the days of McKinley the chauvinistic elements of American society gained the upper hand. This anti-imperialist outlook has led to the search for scapegoats who could be held responsible for the war. Some have blamed Mahan, Roosevelt, Lodge, and the "expansionists"; others have singled out the Hearst and Pulitzer newspapers, crusading Protestantism, and the changing mood of the American people. All have necessarily presupposed that McKinley was driven into the war by forces he found too strong to resist.

The assumption that the United States had no good case for going to war with Spain is at least open to question, whether regarded from considerations of morality or the national interest. But the assumptions that McKinley had no policy of his own or that domestic politics influenced his actions more than his assessment of America's international interests do not seem justified by the evidence.

No penetrating contemporary assessment of McKinley's character has survived. He rarely revealed his innermost thoughts, though his manner was friendly and easy. Few people talked to him without feeling the better for it. He listened courteously to many and diverse opinions and gave the impression of agreeing with everyone. He was "a bit of a jollier," as Roosevelt was quick to observe. There is no denying that on occasion he rather overstepped the mark. When, for example, in the autumn of 1898 he assured a group of visiting clergymen that the decision to retain the Philippines had come to him one night in answer to his prayers, his visitors no doubt accepted the tale at its face value. In fact the President's attitude on the Philippine question had been evolving for months without celestial assistance. McKinley simply could not resist presenting his policy in a light calculated to charm his audience.

A year earlier, in speaking to Theodore Roosevelt, McKinley adopted a very different tone. Roosevelt had just delivered a bellicose speech to the Naval War College proclaiming, "no triumph of peace is quite so great as the supreme triumph of war." Secretary of the Navy John D. Long was shocked, but the President complimented Roosevelt and assured him "that he had read every word of [the speech] and heartily endorsed it." McKinley made everyone who came to see him feel that his views were of particular interest; he gave the impression of being easily influenced by others; yet, in fact, he considered advice critically. McKinley had discovered that flattery usually worked where outspoken opposition served no useful purpose. He was as straightforward as an adroit president could afford to be.

McKinley was very much a product of the Victorian age. He never doubted that the path of righteousness would be revealed to those who sought it; he did not hesitate to form his own judgments, and he clung to his decisions with obduracy. He was extraordinarily self-reliant, and this was the source both of his strength and weakness. In ordering his personal life and in framing his policies, he followed simple moral precepts that may strike the modern ear as banal; the most important of the self-imposed rules was the need to do one's duty. He would share with no one the responsibility of making decisions.

The charge of McKinley's weakness is justified on the ground that he failed to take a more decided public stand on the Cuban issue in the face of the uncompromising attitude of Congress and of the majority of the American people. The President, "who is now in the rear, will go to the front. He shivers a little, but he will go," wrote the fiery Senator Chandler on the eve of the war. But McKinley was perfectly aware that his popularity was on the decline. As the excitement in February and March 1898 reached fever pitch, he even feared that his efforts to reach a peaceful solution would expose him to personal danger. His drives in Washington became infrequent, and he confided to Long his foreboding of assassination. But this did not deter the President from following the path of duty as he conceived it. We may reach the conclusion that, since his policy failed, the President was mistaken: that he would have done better to take the people more into his confidence, that his methods were faulty, and that his sense of right and wrong did not necessarily settle the ethical issues involved for all time. Even so, it is difficult to justify the assertion that McKinley's diplomacy lacked political or personal courage.

McKinley kept his own counsel and, with the help of the Assistant Secretary of State, Judge William Rufus Day, retained control of the conduct of foreign relations. He surrounded himself with a rather second-rate Cabinet. One member, Secretary of State John Sherman, was rapidly declining in senility, while Long, Secretary of the Navy, suffered from nervous troubles. Such an Administration suited the President; he rarely consulted his colleagues on questions of importance. His Cabinet councils were little more than jolly social gatherings. "Cabinet meeting this morning," Secretary Long noted in his journal on February 4, 1898, "like most of our cabinet meetings, it amounts to little: most of the time devoted to chatting about personal matters." But political necessity obliged McKinley to take into his confidence a group of congressional leaders, the caucus of senators and congressmen who supported him on Capitol Hill.

During the periods when Congress was in session, there was always the danger that precipitate action might impede the President's diplomacy. McKinley was convinced that time was of the essence if the Spanish government were to be encouraged to settle the Cuban question. He recognized that to expect the proud Spaniard to capitulate within the space of a few weeks was asking for the impossible. The difficulty was to win the necessary breathing space when the Cuban crisis had already dragged on for two years.

In his inaugural address, McKinley appealed to the country for calm. He declared his intention to settle the tragic and complicated Cuban problem by diplomacy.

It will be our aim to pursue a firm and dignified foreign policy, which shall be just, impartial, ever watchful of our national honor, and always insisting upon the enforcement of the lawful rights of American citizens everywhere. Our diplomacy should seek nothing more and nothing less than is due us. We want no wars of conquest; we must avoid the temptation of territorial aggression. Wars should never be entered upon until every agency of peace has failed; peace is preferable to war in almost every contingency.

These words may have a platitudinous ring, but McKinley was in fact defining what he regarded as his path of duty. If the war in Cuba could be brought to an end without the armed intervention of the United States—and so without the loss of American lives—then it was the duty of the President to make every effort to strive for peace. . . .

The mood of Congress at the time of McKinley's inauguration left little room for optimistic illusions. Despite Senator Lodge's plea that the Administration should be given the "opportunity to inform itself with the utmost thoroughness as to the conditions" existing in Cuba before being asked to act, a resolution to recognize Cuban belligerency, introduced by Senator Morgan of Pennsylvania, passed the Senate in May 1897. It was rejected by the House. McKinley now anxiously waited for Congress to adjourn before he embarked on an active Cuban policy. He hoped to present the nation with the fruits of his diplomacy in the interval before Congress met again in December. He would have liked to convince all but the irreconcilable minority that the Cuban conflict could be resolved without resort to war.

*   *   *

As the year 1897 drew to a close, McKinley had already achieved much. A number of senators were in sympathy with Lodge's plea that the President should be left more time to work out his own policy. But the majority of Democrats opposed him, as did some bellicose Republicans. The President could

nevertheless be satisfied that he had so far kept the legislature in check and was
handling the situation well. In his annual message to Congress that December he
outlined the Administration's policy. He avoided detailed proposals; he
asserted Spain must be left more time to work out the reforms on which it had
now irrevocably embarked; but should the strife be prolonged, the
Administration would decide on its course in accordance with "its own high
sense of right and in consonance with the dearest interests and convictions of our
own people." It all seemed vague, a mere repetition of what had already been
said many times and for several years. If, however, McKinley's public statements
are read along with his secret diplomatic communications to [Ambassador
Stewart] Woodford, there is no mistaking the President's determination to make
it clear to the Spaniards that they could no longer evade the real issue: to
establish without delay conditions of lasting peace in Cuba. In a long note on
December 20, 1897, McKinley encouraged the Liberal government to persevere
on the part of reform in Cuba: "Spain has entered upon a pathway from
which no backward step is possible." He bluntly asserted that the previous
Conservative policy of attempting to crush the Cubans by force was doomed to
failure. He attempted to dissociate the Spanish government from the actions
of its predecessor in office. Since the Spanish preferred to give assurances that
peace would be brought to Cuba by Spain's own efforts, the United States
for its part was ready to wait in "kindly expectancy . . . so long as the event shall
invite and justify that course." Despite the friendly tone, the Spanish
ministers were painfully aware that McKinley had not departed from his
original demands.

*   *   *

Early in March the President sent fresh instructions to Woodford. He stressed
that his requirements for a settlement of the Cuban question had not changed
since the previous December. He also observed that the Spanish attempt to make
autonomy workable on the island had failed, that the distress on the island
continued unabated, and that the Spanish Army had won no successes. Three
weeks later the President, through Woodford, warned the royal government
that unless he could assure Congress that peace would be established on the
island, he would have to lay the whole question before Congress. The
legislature would very likely pass resolutions recognizing Cuban independence.

Throughout that month McKinley attempted to reassure the European
ambassadors in Washington that his intentions were pacific, to convince the
government in Madrid that a Cuban settlement could no longer be delayed, and
to restrain Congress from taking precipitous action. His message early in
March requesting $50 million for the national defense calmed senatorial fears
that the President might act less vigorously than they hoped. Then on March 27,
McKinley transmitted the report on the *Maine* to Congress, accompanied by a
mild message. The loyal and hardworking senators who supported the
Administration now warned McKinley that they could not control Congress
much longer.

The time for decision had come. McKinley enumerated his conditions for peace with Spain after consulting a number of leading Republican senators. He made two distinct proposals on two successive days. The first he sent on March 26. It was based on the assumption that the Spanish government was willing to open direct negotiations with the insurgent leaders. If the Spanish ministers preferred to negotiate with the Cubans, then only a Spanish offer of "full self-government" (which meant independence, Day telegraphed two days later) would, in the President's opinion, afford a reasonable guarantee of peace. He added that he would be willing to aid in the restoration of peace on this basis. McKinley's alternative proposal (it will be recalled that the President had left to Spain a choice of two different ways of settling the Cuban question since the previous summer) was sent to Madrid on March 27. It was based on the assumption that the Spanish government was not prepared to offer the insurgents independence straightway. Since, if that were the case, any Spanish attempt to initiate negotiations with the Cuban leaders would be abortive, McKinley insisted that he would be able to persuade the Cubans to lay down their arms only if Spain were ready to accept his mediation and grant an armistice until October 1. McKinley hoped that, if the terms of peace had not been agreed upon before the expiration of the armistice, Spain would also agree to his acting as final arbiter. He did not make this condition a sine qua non. McKinley made it clear that he expected the Spanish to take immediate steps to relieve the distress of the Cuban people, whichever alternative Spain decided to accept—direct negotiations on the basis of independence or American mediation and an armistice.

There was not the slightest chance that Spain would accept either proposition. Immediate independence was out of the question; to invite the mediation of the American President was unthinkable. The Spanish ministers did eventually grant an armistice, but its duration was conditional; an armistice by itself, even if unconditional, did not in any case meet the President's requirements. In Madrid, Ambassador Woodford was rapidly getting out of his depth.

In February Woodford had been in despair; he had reported to McKinley and Day that no further concessions were to be expected from Spain. The Queen would rather fight the United States over Cuba than endanger the dynasty by handing Cuba to the Cubans, thereby exposing her son, the King, and herself, as Regent, to the wrath of the people. But during March Woodford believed that a settlement could be reached; Moret had evidently convinced him of Spain's sincerity. Woodford met the leading members of the Spanish government and began to sympathize with them in their dilemma. They would, he thought, move forward as fast as their sense of pride could permit them. He therefore did not give up his hope of peace even when, on March 31, the Spanish insisted that an armistice could be granted only if the insurgents asked for it. The Spanish ministers, he surmised correctly, had not yet said the last word. Woodford believed that the obstacles to peace were more matters of form than of substance. "It has turned, as I feared, on a question of punctilio. Spanish pride will not permit the Ministry to propose and offer an armistice," Woodford wrote to the President on the last day of March. If he could secure an armistice, he assured McKinley and Day, then the fighting on the island would end permanently and Cuba would become the property of the United States. Woodford's optimism and desire to reduce the President's alternatives to a single condition, a Spanish proclamation of an armistice, aroused misgivings in Washington. Did Woodford really grasp his instructions precisely? On April 3, Day reminded the Ambassador in Madrid that the President could make no new suggestions. He also explained that a Spanish proclamation of armistice would not suffice: "An armistice involves an agreement between Spain and insurgents which must be voluntary on the part of each, and if accepted by them would make for peace. . . . An armistice to be effective, must be immediately proffered and accepted by insurgents." As for the peace Woodford had written he was confident of being able to secure, was Spain ready to give Cuba her independence?

Day's warnings had no effect; Woodford's desire for peace was so ardent that he began to believe what he wanted to believe: time and patience would lead all sides to an acceptable solution; the Spanish government might be induced to proclaim an armistice. No more than that—but Woodford thought that if Spain took this step, peace for Cuba would be secure. In Washington, McKinley took a more realistic view, although the President did not give up hope that Spain would meet all his essential conditions. On April 5, Woodford telegraphed that the Queen, at the behest of the Pope, was considering the proclamation of an armistice to last until October. Four days later he was able to report triumphantly that an armistice had actually been granted at the request of the Pope and the great powers. Now Spain should not be humiliated: "You will win the fight on your own lines," Woodford advised the President. . . .

Senator Spooner, who complained "the world does not know what war is today, with the modern arms, projectiles and death-dealing instrumentalities," described the Senate proceedings during the last days of peace. "Apparently Congress cannot keep its head. It looks at this time of writing as if a majority had their watches out, waiting for the arrival of a particular hour on Monday, to force the hand of the President, and let loose the dogs of war. I have with others, done all in my power thus far to give the President time to work out the delicate and difficult negotiations which he has in hand. I have believed that he, if let alone, could pull through . . . The situation is calculated to make a man distrust our system a little bit."

The Spanish reply reached Washington on April 10. The European ambassadors in Washington then believed—and the same view has frequently, but erroneously, been expressed since—that Spain had capitulated to McKinley at the eleventh hour. In fact the Spanish government rejected the President's terms. An armistice was proclaimed, but only "for such length of time" as the Spanish commander-in-chief "may think prudent to prepare and facilitate the peace earnestly desired by all." It was not a just armistice. The Cubans were asked to stop fighting for as long as the Spanish commander-in-chief thought it convenient and were offered autonomy. When Day asked the Spanish Minister whether Spain was ready to grant Cuba independence if the President considered it necessary, the Minister said "No." In short, the armistice was of no practical value; the Cuban leaders were certain to reject the demand to cease their struggle on Spain's terms just at the time when they believed they were winning their fight for independence. Peace on the island had not been brought one step closer. The Spanish ministers also remained adamant in refusing the President's mediation.

On April 11, McKinley sent his message to Congress. It did not close the door to a negotiated settlement and was so worded, Day cabled Woodford, as to ensure some days of congressional debate. It may be well asked why the President hesitated even in mid-April 1898 to lead the nation boldly to war. He evidently thought there was a chance that, faced with an ultimatum—for that was what he had delivered by leaving the decision of war to a bellicose Congress—Spain might still yield. He could, after all, look back on six months of negotiations during which Spain had, in the face of unremitting pressure (and frequently at the last moment), made concessions such as few sovereign states have ever made in times of peace. It seemed as if Spain had to take only one more step to settle the crisis. But in Madrid, this one step—willingness to grant Cuba its independence if no other solution could be found—no Spanish minister was ready to take. Recognition of Cuban independence was not regarded as just one more concession: the maintenance of Spanish sovereignty over Cuba was the one condition which the Spanish ministry would not yield, whatever other concessions might be wrung from its government. This was the final obstacle to peace. McKinley's message to Congress had gained eight more days for the Spanish government, but all to no avail, and when war came McKinley was prepared.

The President would have been ready to see Cuba pass into the hands of a government chosen by the Cubans if thereby a war could have been avoided. But once he had gone to war, McKinley would cause the Cuban settlement to coincide with the long-term interests of the United States. Many knowledgeable Americans doubted whether the Cubans were really ready for self-government and feared that immediate independence would create fresh problems for the United States. McKinley shared these fears and inclined to the view that the Cubans would first have to pass through a period of American tutelage before they could be trusted to make wise use of a representative government. It had never been part of McKinley's policy to recognize the Junta leaders as the lawful government of Cuba. No more was it part of his policy to do so in the early days of April. His message of April 11 advised Congress not to recognize the insurgent regime and merely expressed his eventual intention to recognize an independent Cuban government.

While a large majority of the House was ready to grant the President the power and discretion he was asking for, the Senate was less docile. A group of idealistic Democrats, who looked upon war with Spain as a holy crusade for the sake of the Cubans, combined with a group of Republicans, led by Foraker of Ohio, who suspected that McKinley would even now wriggle out of a declaration of war. They added to the resolutions reported by the Senate Foreign Relations Committee a clause recognizing "the Republic of Cuba as the true and lawful government of that island." The Senate also adopted the now famous Teller amendment, disclaiming any intention on the part of the United States to exercise control over the island. Once Cuba was pacified, the government of the island was to be left to the people of Cuba. Although the House-Senate conference committee subsequently struck out the provision requiring the immediate recognition of the insurgent government, a compromise was reached only at the price of leaving the Teller amendment untouched. To this extent, McKinley's hands were tied, and the Administration did not enter the war entirely free from commitment. The amendment thus represented a defeat of Administration policies, but it is doubtful whether in fact the will of Congress very much affected McKinley's subsequent Cuban policy. Nor had congressional pressure before the war influenced the President's policy as much as has been supposed. He had been following a purposeful Cuban policy since July 1897.

We now know there was only one possible end—war. Short of Cuban independence, there could have been no Spanish-Cuban settlement, and the Spanish government was not ready to grant independence. McKinley was searching for an alternative where there was none.

For nine months McKinley steadily increased the pressure in Madrid. His notes to Spain were clear and unequivocal. If Spain could not bring peace to Cuba then the United States would do so—if possible by diplomacy, if necessary by war. He had threatened to leave the Cuban decision to Congress, in this way hoping to induce the Spanish government to accept his terms. As long as McKinley believed that his policies might succeed, he skillfully held Congress back—even after the disaster to the *Maine*. No President before had been faced with such a weight of public opinion in favor of war, encouraged as it was by a sensational press, making use of the added effectiveness of mass circulation. The President's messages to Congress were designed to calm the rising hysteria; his notes to Spain were meant to convince the royal government that the time for words and promises had passed and that only the restoration of peace in Cuba could stop American intervention. Evidence suggests that McKinley's policy was steadily moving to the point where he would have presented an ultimatum to Spain quite independently of the *Maine* disaster. The jingoes believed that they had driven McKinley into war, de Lôme thought the President was weak and easily influenced by public opinion, and Roosevelt felt that he had no more backbone than a chocolate eclair. While the roles these men played in the crisis of 1898 have generally been condemned, their judgment of McKinley has not been questioned. McKinley had to make clear his Cuban policies in the instructions he sent to Madrid, and the reconstructed story shows neither weakness nor indecision.

For more than two nerve-racking months, McKinley had strained party loyalty to the limit, courted widespread unpopularity, allowed the impression to prevail that he was indecisive, unable to lead the nation, and abdicating leadership to Congress. The methods of his diplomacy required this sacrifice. The risk of unpopularity did not deflect the President from doing his duty as he conceived it. These are not the actions of a man lacking character or political courage. The inflexibility of both McKinley and the Spanish was the ultimate cause of war. The President would not deviate from his duty to the Cubans. He profoundly believed that the United States could no longer avoid war; the dictates of civilization and humanity impelled her to act. The Spanish ministers denied the United States any voice in the settlement of Spain's internal problems.

They based their contention on the accepted standards of international conduct. Both sides believed that they had shown great patience and forbearance. And so President McKinley and the Queen Regent of Spain went to war in 1898, each firmly convinced of the righteousness of the cause.

six
the hesitancy
of american
business

JULIUS W. PRATT

*The question of the influence of American business in the
United States remains one of the most divisive issues in
American history. Julius W. Pratt (b. 1888), emeritus
professor of history, State University of New York at
Buffalo, tackled the question in the 1930s, when business
was unpopular because of the Depression and charges by
many commentators, including Senator Gerald P. Nye and
his investigating committee, that businessmen had
devilishly shoved America into World War I. By studying
imperialism in the late nineteenth century, Pratt hoped to
dispel the notion of conspiratorial and expansionist
businessmen. In his* Expansionists of 1898 (1936), *Pratt
denied that American business had been responsible for the
Spanish-American War and the preparatory expansionist
policies. Until William A. Williams, Thomas J. McCormick,
and Walter LaFeber, among others, offered contrasting
evidence, demonstrating that business was, if anything,
divided, Pratt's thesis dominated history textbooks.
Williams went beyond Pratt to argue that what was
important was not direct business pressure, but a world view
of economic expansion shared by most leaders. Pratt's*
Expansionists of 1898 *constituted the Shaw Lectures some
twenty years before Howard K. Beale delivered his.
Pratt has also written* Expansionists of 1812 (1925),
America's Colonial Experiment (1950), *and* Cordell Hull
(1964).

Source: Julius W. Pratt, *Expansionists of 1898: The Acquisition of
Hawaii and the Spanish Islands* (Baltimore: The Johns Hopkins
Press, 1936), pp. 233–39, 243–46, 248–57, 266–67, 272–74, 278.
Copyright 1936 by The Johns Hopkins Press. Used by permission of
the publisher.

We may begin with a generalization, the evidence for which will be presented as the chapter proceeds. American business, in general, had strongly opposed action that would lead to war with Spain. American business had been either opposed or indifferent to the expansionist philosophy which had arisen since 1890. But almost at the moment when the war began, a large section of American business had, for reasons that will become apparent, been converted to the belief that a program of territorial expansion would serve its purposes. Hence business, in the end, welcomed the "large policy" and exerted its share of pressure for the retention of the Spanish islands and such related policies as the annexation of Hawaii and the construction of an isthmian canal.

One public man to whom the welfare of American business was of so much concern that he may almost be considered its spokesman in the Senate, was McKinley's friend, Mark Hanna. No one was more unwilling than he to see the United States drift into war with Spain. To Hanna, in the words of his biographer, "the outbreak of war seemed to imperil the whole policy of domestic economic amelioration which he placed before every other object of political action." Hanna's attitude appears to have been identical with that of leading business men. This conclusion is based not only upon the few published biographies of such men, but also upon the study of a large number of financial and trade periodicals, of the proceedings of chambers of commerce and boards of trade, and of material in the *Miscellaneous Files* of the Department of State, containing numerous letters and petitions from business men and organizations.

That business sentiment, especially in the East, was strongly anti-war at the close of 1897 and in the opening months of 1898, is hardly open to doubt. Wall Street stocks turned downward whenever the day's news seemed to presage war and climbed again with information favorable to peace. Bulls and bears on the market were those who anticipated, respectively, a peaceable and a warlike solution of the Cuban question. The "jingo," in Congress or the press, was an object of intense dislike to the editors of business and financial journals, who sought to counteract his influence by anti-war editorials in their columns. Boards of trade and chambers of commerce added their pleas for the maintenance of peace to those of the business newspapers and magazines. So marked, indeed, was the anti-war solidarity of the financial interests and their spokesmen that the jingoes fell to charging Wall Street with want of patriotism. Wall Street, declared the Sacramento *Evening Bee* (March 11, 1898), was "the colossal and aggregate Benedict Arnold of the Union, and the syndicated Judas Iscariot of humanity." Senator Thurston, of Nebraska, charged that opposition to war was found only among the "money-changers," bringing from the editor of *The American Banker* the reply that "there is not an intelligent, self-respecting and civilized American citizen anywhere who would not prefer to have the existing crisis culminate in peaceful negotiations."

* * *

The reasons for this attitude on the part of business are not far to seek.

Since the panic of 1893 American business had been in the doldrums. Tendencies toward industrial revival had been checked, first by the Venezuela war scare in December, 1895, and again by the free silver menace in 1896. But in 1897 began a real revival, and before the end of the year signs of prosperity appeared on all sides. The New York *Commercial* conducted a survey of business conditions in a wide variety of trades and industries, from which it concluded that, "after three years of waiting and of false starts, the groundswell of demand has at last begun to rise with a steadiness which leaves little doubt that an era of prosperity has appeared." January, 1898, said the same article, is "a supreme moment in the period of transition from depression to comparative prosperity." This note of optimism one meets at every turn, even in such a careful and conservative sheet as the *Commercial and Financial Chronicle*. As early as July, 1897, this paper remarked: "We appear to be on the eve of a revival in business"; and in December after remarking upon the healthy condition of the railroads and the iron industry, it concluded: "In brief, no one can study the industrial conditions of today in America without a feeling of elation. . . ." The *Wall Street Journal* found only two "blue spots" in the entire country: Boston, which suffered from the depressed demand for cotton goods, and New York, where senseless rate cutting by certain railroads caused uneasiness. "Throughout the west, southwest and on the Pacific coast business has never been better, nor the people more hopeful."

A potent cause for optimism was found in the striking expansion of the American export trade. A volume of exports far in excess of those of any recent year, a favorable balance of trade of $286,000,000, and an especially notable increase in exports of manufactures of iron, steel, and copper, convinced practically every business expert that the United States was on the point of capturing the markets of the world. "There is no question," said one journal, "that the world, generally, is looking more and more to the United States as the source of its supply for very many of the staple commodities of life." Especially elated were spokesmen of the iron and steel industry. Cheaper materials and improved methods were enabling the American producer to undersell his British competitor in Europe and in the British possessions, and Andrew Carnegie was talking of a great shipbuilding yard near New York to take advantage of these low costs. The *Iron Age,* in an editorial on "The Future of Business," foretold the abolition of the business cycle by means of a better planned economy, consolidation of railroads and industries, reduction of margins of profit, higher wages, and lower prices to consumers.

To this fair prospect of a great business revival the threat of war was like a spectre at the feast. A foreign complication, thought the *Commercial and Financial Chronicle* in October, 1897, would quickly mar "the trade prosperity which all are enjoying." Six months later (April 2, 1898), after a discussion of the effect of war rumors on the stock exchange, it declared: ". . . Every influence has been, and even now is, tending strongly towards a term of decided prosperity, and that the Cuban disturbance, and it alone, has arrested the movement and checked enterprise."

* * *

Something of a freak among New York financial journals was the *Financial Record,* which, in November, 1897, denounced "the cowardice of our Administration in refusing the phenomenally brave Cubans the commonest rights of belligerency" as "a disgrace to the United States," and argued that war with Spain, far from depressing securities or injuring business, "would vastly increase the net earning power of every security sold on our market today." The mystery of this jingo attitude is explained when we discover that this journal had been a warm advocate of the free coinage of silver.

Business opinion in the West, especially in the Mississippi Valley, appears to have been less opposed to war and less apprehensive of its results than that of the Atlantic coast. The Kansas City Board of Trade, at the beginning of 1897, had urged recognition of Cuban independence. The Cincinnati Chamber of Commerce, at a meeting on March 29, 1898, adopted "amidst much enthusiasm," resolutions condemning Spain for cruelties to the Cubans and the destruction of the "Maine" and calling for a "firm and vigorous policy which will have for its purpose—peacefully if we can, but with force if we must—the redress of past wrongs, and the complete and unqualified independence of Cuba." The Chicago *Economist* denied that war would seriously hurt business or endanger the gold standard and asserted that the liberation of Cuba, by peace or war, would mean another star of glory for the United States and would produce "results of the highest value to mankind." The *Rand-McNally Bankers' Monthly,* of the same city, while opposing war, called attention to the fact that while the war scare had demoralized the stock market, "general business activity apparently received an impetus." Similarly the *Age of Steel* (St. Louis), while much preferring peace, "when not secured at the price of national honor," comforted its readers with the thought that although foreign trade might suffer, home trade and industries would be stimulated by war. . . .

Even in New York, business men saw some rays of light piercing the war clouds. Stock market operators, according to the *Wall Street Journal,* just after the "Maine" explosion, "did not look for any great break in the market, because actual war with Spain would be a very small affair compared with the Venezuela complication with Great Britain." Their expectation was for a drop in stocks at the beginning of hostilities, followed by a resumption of the recent advance. In fact, the first shock might well be followed by a boom. "The nation looks for peace," declared *Dun's Review,* March 5, "but knows that its sources of prosperity are quite beyond the reach of any attack that is possible." *Bradstreet's* contrasted the jumpiness of Wall Street over war news with "the calm way in which general business interests have regarded the current foreign complications," and *Dun's Review* of March 12 stated that no industry or branch of business showed any restriction, while some had been rapidly gaining, that railroads were increasing their profits while speculators sold their stocks, and that there was a growing demand for the products of all the great industries.

Despite such expressions as these, there seems little reason to question the belief that an overwhelming preponderance of the vocal business interests of the country strongly desired peace. By the middle of March, however, many organs of business opinion were admitting that a war with Spain might bring no serious disaster, and there was a growing conviction that such a war was inevitable. . . .

It remains to examine the attitude of certain American business men and corporations having an immediate stake in Cuba, or otherwise liable to be directly affected by American intervention. Much American capital, as is well known, was invested in the Cuban sugar industry. Upon this industry the civil war fell with peculiarly devastating effect, not only cutting off profits on capital so invested, but also crippling a valuable carrying trade between Cuba and the United States. Naturally enough, some firms suffering under these conditions desired to see the United States intervene to end the war, though such intervention might lead to war between the United States and Spain. In May, 1897, a memorial on the subject bearing over three hundred signatures was presented to John Sherman, Secretary of State. The signers described themselves as "citizens of the United States, doing business as bankers, merchants, manufacturers, steamship owners and agents in the cities of Boston, New York, Philadelphia, Baltimore, Savannah, Charleston, Jacksonville, New Orleans, and other places, and also other citizens of the United States, who have been for many years engaged in the export and import trade with the Island of Cuba." They called attention to the serious losses to which their businesses had been subjected by the hostilities in Cuba and expressed the hope that, in order to prevent further loss, to reestablish American commerce, and also to secure "the blessings of peace for one and a half millions of residents of the Island of Cuba now enduring unspeakable distress and suffering," the United States Government might take steps to bring about an honorable reconciliation between the parties to the conflict.

Another memorial, signed by many of the same subscribers, was presented to President McKinley on February 9, 1898, by a committee of New York business men. It asserted that the Cuban war, which had now continued for three entire years, had caused an average loss of $100,000,000 a year, or a total loss of $300,000,000 in the import and export trade between Cuba and the United States, to which were to be added "heavy sums irretrievably lost by the destruction of American properties, or properties supported by American capital in the Island itself, such as sugar factories, railways, tobacco plantations, mines and other industrial enterprises; the loss of the United States in trade and capital by means of this war being probably far greater and more serious than that of all the other parties concerned, not excepting Spain herself."

The sugar crop of 1897–1898, continued the memorial, appeared for the most part lost like its two predecessors, and unless peace could be established before May or June of the current year, the crop of 1898–1899, with all the business dependent upon it, would likewise be lost, since the rainy season of summer and fall would be required "to prepare for next winter's crop, by repairing damaged fields, machinery, lines of railways, &c." In view of the importance to the United States of the Cuban trade and of American participation "in the ownership or management of Cuban sugar factories, railways and other enterprises," the petitioners hoped that the President would deem the situation "of sufficient importance as to warrant prompt and efficient measures by our Government, with the sole object of restoring peace . . . and with it restoring to us a most valuable commercial field."

How much weight such pressure from special interests had with the

administration there is no way of knowing. But it is to be noted that the
pressure from parties directly interested was not all on one side. Mr. E. F.
Atkins, an American citizen who divided his time between Boston and his
sugar plantation of Soledad near Cienfuegos, Cuba, which he had developed at
a cost of $1,400,000, had been able, through protection received from the Spanish
Government and through a corps of guards organized and paid by himself, to
continue operations throughout the period of the insurrection. He was
frequently in Washington, where he had influential friends, during both the
Cleveland and McKinley administrations and worked consistently against
the adoption of any measures likely to provoke war.

Unlike some of the sugar plantations, American-owned iron mines in Cuba
continued to do active business despite the insurrection. Three American iron and
manganese enterprises in the single province of Santiago claimed to have an
investment of some $6,000,000 of purely American capital, a large proportion
of which was in property which could easily be destroyed. "We are fully
advised as to our status in case of war," wrote the representative of one company
to the Assistant Secretary of State, "and that this property might be subject to
confiscation or destruction by the Spanish Government." War between Spain and
the United States, wrote the president of another company, "will very likely
mean the destruction of our valuable plant and in any event untold loss to
our Company and its American stockholders." An American cork company with
large interests in Spain; a New York merchant with trade in the Mediterranean
and Black Sea; a Mobile firm which had chartered a Spanish ship to carry a
cargo of timber—these are samples of American business interests which saw in
war the threat of direct damage to themselves. They are hardly offset by the
high hopes of an enterprising gentleman of Norfolk, "representing a party of
capitalists who are enthusiastic supporters of the Government," who applied to
the State Department for a letter of marque "to enable us to lawfully capture
Spanish merchant vessels and torpedo boats," adding: "We have secured
option on a fine steam vessel, and on receipt of proper documents will put to
sea forth with."

It seems safe to conclude, from the evidence available, that the only
important business interests (other than the business of sensational journalism)
which clamored for intervention in Cuba were those directly or indirectly
concerned in the Cuban sugar industry; that opposed to intervention were the
influence of other parties (including at least one prominent sugar planter)
whose business would suffer direct injury from war and also the overwhelming
preponderance of general business opinion. After the middle of March, 1898,
some conservative editors came to think intervention inevitable on humanitarian
grounds, but many of the most influential business journals opposed it to the end.

We can now turn to the question whether American business was imperialistic;
whether, in other words, business opinion favored schemes for acquiring foreign
territory to supply it with markets, fields for capital investment, or commercial
and naval stations in distant parts of the world. American business men were
not unaware of the struggle for colonies then raging among European nations.
Did they feel that the United States ought to participate in that struggle?

We have seen above that the rising tide of prosperity was intimately connected

with the increase in American exports, particularly of manufactured articles.
That the future welfare of American industry was dependent upon the
command of foreign markets was an opinion so common as to appear almost
universal. The New York *Journal of Commerce* pointed out, early in 1897, that
the nation's industrial plant had been developed far beyond the needs of
domestic consumption. In the wire nail industry there was said to be machinery
to make four times as many nails as the American markets could consume.
Rail mills, locomotive shops, and glass factories were in a similar situation.
"Nature has thus destined this country for the industrial supremacy of the world,"
said the same paper later in the year. When the National Association of
Manufacturers met in New York for its annual convention in January, 1898,
"the discussion of ways and means for extending this country's trade, and
more particularly its export business, was, in fact, almost the single theme of the
speakers," according to *Bradstreet's,* which added the comment: "Nothing is
more significant of the changed attitude toward this country's foreign trade,
manifested by the American manufacturer today as compared with a few years
ago, than the almost single devotion which he pays to the subject of possible
export-trade extension."

   But if business men believed, prior to the opening of the war with Spain,
that foreign markets were to be secured through the acquisition of colonies, they
were strangely silent about it. To the program of colonial expansion which
for almost a decade had been urged by such men as Mahan, Albert Shaw, Lodge,
Roosevelt, and Morgan, business had remained, to all appearances, either
indifferent or antagonistic. To the business man, such a program was merely
one form of dangerous jingoism. A large section of business opinion had,
indeed, favored plans for the building of a Nicaraguan canal with governmental
assistance, and some spokesmen for business had favored annexation of the
Hawaiian Islands. But beyond these relatively modest projects few business
men, apparently, wished to go. . . .*

   Colonies were not only certain to bear a fruit of danger and expense; they
were valueless from the commercial point of view. Did not the colonies of
Great Britain afford us one of the most valuable of our export markets? Did we
not trade as advantageously with Guiana, a British colony, as with independent
Venezuela? "Most of our ideas of the commercial value of conquests, the
commercial uses of navies and the commercial advantages of political control,"
said the New York *Journal of Commerce,* dated back to times when colonial
policies were designed to monopolize colonial trade for the mother country. The
Commercial and Financial Chronicle believed that the current European
enthusiasm for colonies was based on false premises; for although trade often

---

* Exceptions to this general rule were the *Financial Record,* which was pro-war (as shown
above) and which also hailed the prospect of colonial responsibilities (June 23, 1897,
March 23, 1898); and the New York *Commercial,* which thought the United States
should not only annex Cuba and Puerto Rico but should also buy St. Thomas from
Denmark for a naval station (March 31, April 8, 1898). The *American Banker,* in
April, 1898, thought it would be good business to buy Cuba, pay for it in silver, and
set it up as an American protectorate. It remarked: "A nation that borrows foreign capital,
and in fact mortgages its resources to foreigners, must expect when it becomes unable to
pay to be interfered with from without."

followed the flag, "the trade is not always with the home markets of the colonizer. England and the United States are quite as apt to slip in with their wares under the very Custom-House pennant of the French or German dependency." Outright opposition, such as this, to the idea of colonial expansion is not common in the business periodicals examined; much more common is complete silence on the subject. Positive and negative evidence together seem to warrant the conclusion that American business in general, at the opening of 1898, was either indifferent to imperialism, or definitely opposed.

* * *

In the light of [the] widespread and intense interest in the preservation of the Chinese market, we can perhaps understand why American business, which had been, to all appearances, anti-war and anti-imperialist, was filled with sudden enthusiasm at the news of Dewey's victory at Manila Bay. Not only did the news dissipate all fears of a long and costly war and send stock prices rapidly upward; still more important, it seemed to place in American hands, all unexpectedly, the key to the trade of the Orient. The attack on the Spanish fleet at Manila had been anticipated for months and well advertised by the American press. Some papers had speculated upon the value of the islands as an American colony and had foreseen that a victory there might greatly alter our relation to the imbroglio in China. But for most, this thought did not occur until arrival of the news that the Spanish fleet was destroyed and Dewey safely in possession of Manila Bay. Then, at last, business men joined the jingoes in their acclaim of imperial conquests. Senator Lodge's exclamation—"We hold the other side of the Pacific, and the value to this country is almost beyond recognition"—was matched by many a formerly conservative business journal. It was not the intrinsic value of the Philippines or their trade that most impressed American writers, though this angle of the subject was not overlooked. Rather, their importance appeared to lie in their position as a gateway to the markets of Eastern Asia.

* * *

It must not be inferred that business opinion was unanimous in favor of retaining the Philippines. There was an undercurrent of opposition or indifference. The New York *Journal of Commerce,* just before the signing of the peace protocol, deplored the fact that timid people were shrinking from imperialism and that "the business men of the country are maintaining a deathlike silence." The *Commercial and Financial Chronicle* was cautious, pointing out that Spain's distant possessions had proved her most vulnerable point—a fact from which the United States might learn a lesson—and hoping that the United States might yet find a way to avoid such a dangerous responsibility. The Baltimore *Journal of Commerce* was, in July, strongly opposed to annexation, and two months later held that no one yet knew whether "our position as wetnurse to Cuba, proprietors of Porto Rico and pantata to the Philippines is likely to bring us profit or loss." The *Iron Age,* which early in the summer had

been strongly for expansion was by September harboring qualms as to the
real value of colonies to the business man. Everett Frazar, president of the
American Asiatic Association, was personally a warm supporter of annexation,
but the Association held upon its table for months without action a resolution on
the subject. The San Francisco *Call,* representing the California and Hawaiian
sugar interests of the Spreckels family, was strongly opposed to annexation,
arguing not only that Anglo Saxons had no aptitude for tropical colonization,
but also frankly warning Californian sugar-beet growers of the danger of
competition from Philippine cane-sugar.

There is no way of measuring accurately the strength of business opinion for
and against the retention of the Philippines. Judging opinion as best we can
from the available expressions of it, it seems safe to conclude that after
the battle of Manila Bay American business became definitely imperialistic—that
is, if a wish to retain the Philippines is an evidence of an imperialistic attitude.
It seems certain, too, from the prominence given to the Chinese situation in
nearly every discussion of the value of the islands, that the conversion of
business opinion was accomplished by the combination of a European threat
against the freedom of the American market in China, present and prospective,
with the dramatic coup of the American fleet in a fine harbor so near the
Chinese coast. In one paper, the New York *Journal of Commerce,* there appears
with beautiful clarity the shift of position induced by the action of the European
Powers in China. In November, 1897, against all schemes of colonial or naval
expansion; in December, for a canal, Hawaii annexation, and a big navy;
in May and thereafter, for retention of the entire Philippine archipelago and
aggressive assertion of American rights in China—the *Journal* reveals a process
of thought which perhaps occurred less clearly and consciously in the minds
of many business men.

*　*　*

American business had yielded reluctantly to the necessity of a war with Spain,
forced upon the United States by popular reaction to the distressing situation in
Cuba. It had not foreseen, or if it foresaw had feared, the colonial responsibilities
to which such a war might lead. But when Dewey's dramatic victory on the
first of May offered a Far Eastern base from which the threatened markets
in China might be defended, it had gladly accepted the result, and long before
the conclusion of peace with Spain, it was building high hopes upon the
supposed opportunities for trade and exploitation in a string of dependencies
stretching from the Philippines to Puerto Rico.

seven
insular
possessions for
the china
market

THOMAS J. McCORMICK

LaFeber wrote that Asia, with its commercial opportunities, was a major part of William Seward's envisioned empire, and Pratt found American businessmen earnest about Asian markets, especially after Dewey's victory at Manila Bay, "the key to the trade of the Orient." Thomas J. McCormick, who now teaches diplomatic history at the University of Wisconsin, where he was once a student of William A. Williams, extends this theme to argue that the Philippines and the China market were intricately linked in the mind of the American elite. McCormick in The China Market *(1967) writes about "informal" empire, whereas LaFeber finds a "new" empire. McCormick compels us to pay attention to definitions, to the link between China and American imperialism, and to the importance of economic factors in diplomacy.*

America's insular acquisitions of 1898 were not products of "large policy" imperialism. Hawaii, Wake, Guam, and the Philippines were not taken principally for their own economic worth, or for their fulfillment of Manifest Destiny, or for their venting of the "psychic crisis." They were obtained, instead, largely in an eclectic effort to construct a system of coaling, cable, and naval stations for an integrated trade route which could help realize America's overriding ambition in the Pacific—the penetration and ultimate domination of the fabled China market.

From the very beginning of the Spanish-American War, the McKinley administration intended to retain a foothold in the Philippines as an "American Hong Kong," a commercial entrepôt to the China market and a center of American military power. Formulation of this policy commitment began seven months before hostilities with Spain, when McKinley examined a Navy Department memorandum written by Assistant Secretary Theodore Roosevelt. This multipurpose paper made one especially bold suggestion: in the event of war with Spain, the Asiatic Squadron "should blockade, and if possible take Manila." Historical myth notwithstanding, it was a suggestion that fell on already prepared ground, for the influential Senator from Connecticut, Orville Platt, had earlier taken pains to impress upon the President "that Manila had become one of the most important ports of the Orient and that the importance of that station demanded most careful attention."

Temporarily put in abeyance by a short-lived détente with Spain in late 1897, the proposal was revived and made the basis of Roosevelt's famous February 25 orders instructing Commodore George Dewey to "start offensive operations in the Philippines" after eliminating the Spanish fleet. The view that this was simply a conspiratorial effort by "large policy" extremists misses two more significant facts: first, Roosevelt's superiors accepted his orders for the Philippine operations even though they unceremoniously countermanded nearly two-thirds of the other miscellaneous orders issued concurrently by the Assistant Secretary; second, the administration had already accepted the substance of Dewey's orders in principle and thereafter permitted the Naval War Board to incorporate the February 25 orders into overall strategy plans for the Pacific. Clearly, while Roosevelt's actions may have been precipitate, they fell within the main lines of the "large policies" of the administration. Of these, Roosevelt, as he privately admitted, was largely "ignorant."

With the outbreak of war the McKinley administration rushed (with almost unseemly haste) to implement its designs upon the likeliest entrepôt, Manila, by determining to send an army of occupation to the Philippine capital. It made this decision on May 2 *before* fully credible news of Dewey's victory at Manila Bay reached Washington and it formally issued the call for Philippine volunteers on May 4, three days *before* an anxious, jittery Secretary of the Navy received authoritative word that the Asiatic Squadron was safe—not immobilized by heavy damages, as he feared. The size of the Army force was to be "not less than twenty thousand men"—quadruple the number recommended by Dewey "to retain [Manila] and thus control the Philippine Islands." It was a move that confirmed Roosevelt in his belief that "the Administration is now fully committed to the large policy." It also persuaded the *San Francisco Chronicle,* on May 4, to splash across its front page the prophetic headline: "WE WILL HOLD THE PHILIPPINES."

On May 11, in one of the most important (and overlooked) decision-making sessions in American history, McKinley and his cabinet gave definite form to their war aims in the Pacific by approving a State Department memorandum calling for Spanish cession to the United States of a suitable "coaling station," presumably Manila. The islands as a whole, however, were to remain with Spain. Acting within the framework of this decision, McKinley on May 19 endowed the commander of the expeditionary force with sufficiently broad powers to effect "the severance of the former political relations of the inhabitants and the establishment of a new political power." Simultaneously, he instructed his Secretary of the Treasury to undertake a study of the islands with an eye "to substitut[ing] new rates and new taxes for those now levied in the Philippines." The stated purpose of both orders, as well as a similar one to Dewey (which he was to "interpret . . . liberally"), was to "[give] to the islands, while in the possession of the United States, that order and security which they have long since ceased to enjoy." Shortly thereafter, on June 3, when it became apparent that the great distance between Manila and Honolulu demanded an intermediate coaling and cable station, the President broadened the American position to include "an island in the Ladrones" (Marianas). The choice made was Guam, and the United States Navy promptly seized it.

As of early June, then, the administration envisioned postwar control only of Manila and Guam as way stations to the orient. But dramatic events swiftly undercut this limited resolve and for a critical fortnight set American policy aimlessly adrift. First of all, as the State Department itself noted, the emergence of the Philippine "insurgents" as "an important factor" made it increasingly doubtful that the islands—minus Manila—could be returned to effective Spanish sovereignty. What then—bestow the largess of Philippine independence but with the stipulation of American control in Manila? Certainly it was within American power to impose such a solution upon the insurgents, by force if necessary. Moreover, the revolutionaries might even have accepted it peacefully, especially since they themselves had offered (as far back as November 1897) to turn over "two provinces and the Custom House at Manila" in exchange for an alliance against Spain (though theoretically these would not be permanent cessions but simply collateral pledges against eventual Filipino repayment for American aid). Nevertheless, relinquishing the rest of the islands ran counter to the administration belief that "if we evacuate, anarchy rules"; (as Dewey later noted) "The natives appear unable to govern."

This presumption that an independent Philippines would be strife-ridden and unstable raised, in turn, the most frightening spectre of all: European intervention, especially by Germany, who considered herself heir-apparent to Spain's insular empire in the Pacific. Actually, the threat was not to American designs on Manila—notwithstanding the Continental feeling that an American foothold in the islands would "complicate the Eastern Question" or the seemingly hostile presence of the German squadron in Manila harbor. Given Germany's diplomatic isolation, Europe's divisiveness, and England's pro-American stance, there was little likelihood of another 1895-type intercession to deprive the victor of his spoils. Germany herself made this clear on several fronts by mid-July. In Berlin one high-ranking German official assured Ambassador White "that Germany does not want large annexations and could not afford to take the Philippine Islands if they were offered her." And in London the German Ambassador told Hay that his government had "no disposition to interfere with,

or deprive [the United States] of [her] rights of conquest in any direction."
It was on the basis of this and other collaborating evidence that Hay advised the
President that he could "now make war or make peace without danger of
disturbing the equilibrium of the world."

The real and continuing danger was German intervention against a weak,
fledgling republic that might well render the isolated American position in
Manila more vulnerable than useful. *This* was no chimera! By mid-June,
Andrew White had already confirmed what the State Department feared: that
Germany would use the expected "anarchy, confusion and insecurity under a
'Philippine Republic' " as an excuse "to secure a stronghold and centre of
influence in that region." Less than a month later, Germany informed White
(and Hay as well) that she expected "a few coaling stations" and "a naval base"
in the Philippines (not to mention control of the Carolines and "predominant"
influence in Samoa). Nor did the passage of time and the solidification of
American intentions eliminate such German ambitions. Even after the
armistice with Spain, rumors flowed freely that Germany still sought "the Sulu
islands" in the southern Philippines—rumors given great credence by
Assistant Secretary of State John Bassett Moore. And in late October the
State Department continued to receive "trustworthy information" that if the
United States failed to take all the Philippines, Germany has "every intention to
establish a foothold there."

Rival intervention or nationalistic revolution: either could undermine
American plans for Manila. Unable to decide on a course of action, American
policy lay momentarily immobilized—at a time when the growing crisis
in China itself least afforded the luxury of prolonged indecision. On the one
hand, intensified rumors that Russia would close Talienwan to foreign
commerce and that she regarded her southern Manchurian leases as "integral
portions of Russian territory" weakened the already shaky underpinnings
of the open door in that key commercial area. At the same time England's
extension of her Hong Kong settlement and her monopolistic approach to
Yangtze Valley developments seemed to indicate that nation's growing
estrangement from her traditional open door approach, and threatened to leave
American policy in China diplomatically isolated. In this deteriorating
framework, any sustained impasse over Philippine policy incurred the risk of
letting American hopes in China go by default. Against the formidable hosts of
Philippine insurgency, German antagonism, and crisis in China, the limited
American policy commitment of June 3 (for Manila and Guam) seemed an
ineffectual one indeed. Realizing the situation, the McKinley administration
in mid-June made a determined effort to break the bind by initiating three
dramatic and interrelated moves in Hawaii, China, and the Philippines,
designed to increase American influence and leverage in the western Pacific. . . .

By early June . . . the Philippine question and the general Far Eastern
situation made it both propitious and imperative that the Hawaiian project be
revived in the hope of strengthening America's hand in the Pacific basin (on the
long-standing belief held by Mahan and many Americans that Hawaii was
the key to "commercial and military control of the Pacific"). The ensuing
debate on the joint congressional resolution was something of a dress rehearsal

for the "great debate" that lay seven months ahead. It was predicated clearly on the assumption that passage of the Hawaiian annexation resolution made retention of the Philippines both possible and likely, while a defeat might foreshadow a similar fate for any territorial aspirations in the oriental archipelago. Congressman William Alden Smith made these and other links explicit with his statement, "If we will take the Hawaiian Islands, hold on to the Philippines, and cultivate good neighborship with the Orient, to which they are the key, the expansion of our commerce will be augmented a thousandfold."

In the actual debate, administration spokesmen hammered the same theme: "we must have Hawaii to help us get our share of China." America needed Hawaii not only for its own economic or cultural worth but also for its commercial and military value as a stepping-stone to the China market. The influential Iowa Representative, William P. Hepburn, captured the theme best when he declared: "I can distinguish between a colonial policy and a commercial policy. I can distinguish between the policy that would scatter colonies all over the islands of the sea and the lands of the earth and that policy which would secure to us simply those facilities of commerce that the new commercial methods make absolutely essential."

* * *

Strikingly, even the opposition accepted the annexationists' chief premise that America needed commercial expansion into Asia. As one Democratic opponent on the House Foreign Affairs Committee put it, he favored "as earnestly as any man can the legitimate extension of our commerce"; nor was he "unmindful that the excessive production of our fields and factories must have an outlet." Some even admitted the modern necessity of commercial-military bases as accoutrements to marketplace expansionism, but they argued that the Pearl Harbor lease of 1886 and the Kiska holding in the Aleutians already gave "all the advantages, everything required." Most, however, stressed the laissez-faire, free-trade approach that "commercial expansion" could best be realized "by competition of quality and price," not by "annexation of territory"; in the words of the Minority Report of the House Foreign Affairs Committee: "Political dominion over the islands is not commercially necessary." But the point did not carry. On June 15 the House passed the annexation resolution by an overwhelming vote, 209 to 91. Three weeks later, after redundant and one-sided discussion (annexationists remained silent to hurry the process), the Senate affirmed the measure by a similar ratio. Thus, on July 8, with McKinley's signature, America acquired her halfway house to the Philippines and China. The acquisition followed by only four days the American occupation of Wake Island, a move intended to meet the technological necessities of an additional cable base between Hawaii and Guam.

Synchronous with the push on Hawaiian annexation, the administration initiated the first step in an American economic offensive in China itself by proposing a government commission to China to recommend measures for trade expansion. Secretary of State William R. Day's supporting letter to Congress made it pointedly clear that an industrial production "of large excess

over home consumption" demanded "an enlargement of foreign markets."
He also made clear his conviction that "American goods have reached a point
of excellence" which made fulfillment of that demand quite feasible. Analyzing
the world market situation, he concluded that underdeveloped areas offered
the best export outlets and that "nowhere is this consideration of more interest
than in its relation to the Chinese Empire." Aware that "the partition of
commercial facilities" in China threatened America's "important interests,"
the Secretary still contended that "the United States . . . is in a position to invite
the most favorable concessions to its industries and trade . . . provided the
conditions are thoroughly understood and proper advantage is taken of
the present situation."

Congress failed to appropriate the necessary monies for the China commercial
commission—as it would again fail in 1899 and 1900. But the chief reason
was most revealing. Most who opposed the measure did so because they
considered such one-shot missions to be ineffectual and an inadequate substitute
for a thoroughgoing reform of our consular representative in China (and
elsewhere as well). Nevertheless, the administration proposal—when coupled
with subsequent prodding of Minister Conger to gain more "Precise
knowledge . . . of the large and grave questions of commercial intercourse," and
with intensive questioning of American consuls as to specific means to expand
the China trade—served clear notice of American intent to take "proper
advantage . . . of the present situation" in order to play a more active role
in China.

Simultaneously, on June 14 the administration capped its trio of dramatic
moves by shelving the earlier decision to return the Philippines to Spain, thus
opening the disposition of the islands to further examination. Thereafter,
despite uneasiness over increased military and administrative burdens, there
began a progressive redefinition of the desired area of American sovereignty:
from Manila, to Luzon, and finally to the entire group. Significantly, this
redefinition involved no real change in the focus of political power; those who
influenced and made policy in June 1898 still did so at year's end. What
changed was men's minds. . . .

In this evolution of Philippine policy, America's commercial stake in China
played the primary role in the thinking of the business and government elite
that chiefly shaped and supported McKinley's decisions. It also played a
significant, though not paramount, part in the outlook of the military advisers
who exercised a more limited but still crucial influence upon the President's
policies.

Between June and October, economic and political leaders united vigorously
in support of retaining all or a large part of the Philippines. But they
de-emphasized the intrinsic worth of the islands and stressed instead their
strategic relationship to China—both as a commercial stepping-stone and a
political-military lever. Moreover, they increasingly affirmed that Manila alone
would not suffice for these purposes, that the United States would have to
take Luzon and perhaps the whole group. In part this support for enlarged
control reflected the already pervasive fear that native revolution or European
penetration might undermine the viability of American power in Manila. But

it also indicated a growing belief, born of newly accumulated information, that
the economic interdependence of the archipelago made efficient division
most difficult. Charles H. Cramp, that renowned Philadelphia shipbuilder,
aptly illustrated the impact of all these factors upon influential Americans when
he asserted: "[Manila] is the emporium and the capital of the Philippines . . .
and it exists because of that fact. . . . Can anyone suppose that with Manila in our
hands and the rest of the Philippine territory under any other Government,
that city would be of any value?

In the business world many associations, journals, and prominent individuals
accepted and propagated the analysis that commercial ambitions in China
demanded American control in the Philippines. Led by the NAM and the
American Asiatic Association, special business organizations urged retention of
the islands "for the protection and furtherance of the commercial interests
of our citizens in the Far East." In a survey of the trade journals of the country,
the *Chicago Inter-Ocean* found it "remarkable with what unanimity they
have advocated the retention of the Philippines." Even more remarkable was
the unanimity of their reasoning: that (in the words of the *Insurance Advocate*)
it would encourage "the teeming millions of the Middle Kingdom" to "buy
largely from us"; that with "one-third of the human race within easy distance
of us, coaling stations on the road, and Manila as the Hong Kong of Uncle Sam's
alert and keen merchant trader," the result was preordained. Finally, save
for a few prominent dissenters like Andrew Carnegie and Chauncey Depew,
McKinley's many personal friends in the corporate world espoused similar
viewpoints. . . .

Most of McKinley's close associates in the federal government (many of
whom were themselves products of the business community) pressed similar
views upon their chief. There were exceptions, of course. Worthington C. Ford,
head of the Bureau of Statistics, appeared to feel (like former Minister to
China George F. Seward) that *"We do not want the Philippines at any price or
under any circumstances."* A few others like Judge Day held largely to the
position (as Carl Schurz summarized it for the President) that "all desirable
commercial facilities" and "all naval stations needed could be secured without
the annexation of populous territories," without "dangerous political
entanglements and responsibilities." But most thought and counseled otherwise.
The redoubtable Mark Hanna, State Department economic expert Frederic
Emory, Charles Denby and his successor Edwin Conger, Comptroller of the
Currency Charles G. Dawes, Assistant Secretary of the Treasury Frank A.
Vanderlip, to name a few, all shared in general the conviction (as Vanderlip
stated) that an American-controlled Philippines would be "pickets of the
Pacific, standing guard at the entrances to trade with the millions of China and
Korea, French Indo-China, the Malay Peninsula, and the islands of Indonesia."
By October, McKinley's cabinet—led by his new Secretary of State, John
Hay—was nearly as one in voicing that sentiment. . . .

Exerting a more narrow influence upon McKinley's Philippine policy was a
third group, the military. In general the President's military advisers shared the
widespread concern over the strategic relationship of the archipelago to
the Asian mainland. Yet, attracted by the siren's call of *imperium* (in which

they would play a prominent role), many military spokesmen also promoted retention of the Philippines as the first step toward an expansive territorial imperialism. These hopes were dashed as McKinley refused to heed their advice for a general American advance into Micronesia and the islands of the South China Sea. But military advice could claim one significant result: it resolved the President's ambivalence (shared by the business and government elite) between taking Luzon or the entire group by convincing him that the islands were an indivisible entity; that strategically and economically they were interdependent and inseparable. Especially persuasive were the lengthy and articulate reports of Commander R. B. Bradford and General Francis V. Greene. Coming in late September and early October, they were a decisive factor in broadening McKinley's instructions. . . .

There can be no doubt that the Chinese question, illuminated by the opinions of business, government, and the military and by the growing crises in China, had a progressive impact upon the shaping of America's Philippine policy. Nowhere is this more dramatically apparent than in the private, candid, and lengthy exchange between McKinley and his peace commissioners at a White House meeting on September 16. The President, speaking somberly and with none of his frequent evasiveness, explained his reasons for retaining all or part of the islands. Almost all of them were negative, embraced with obvious reluctance. The *only* positive and assertive determinant was his conviction that "our tenure in the Philippines" offered the "commercial opportunity" to maintain the open door, a policy which McKinley defined as "no advantages in the Orient which are not common to all." "Asking only the open door for ourselves," he told his commissioners, "we are ready to accord the open door to others." Explaining further, he made it clear that retention of the Philippines was no first step in an orgy of imperialism and jingoism, but simply a limited though important accoutrement to commercial expansion. "The commercial opportunity . . . associated with this opening," he declared, "depends less on large territorial possessions than upon an adequate commercial basis and upon broad and equal privileges."

This last statement was more than mere rhetoric, and nothing proved it more than the President's policy in Micronesia during the last stages of peace negotiations with Spain. Acting on the advice of the Pacific Cable Company that Wake Island had certain technical drawbacks, the administration instructed its peace commissioners to negotiate for the purchase of "one of the Caroline Islands"—preferably Ualan (Kusaie)—"for cable purposes." Despite strong German protests that "Kusaie lies in the midst of German sphere" and that "Germany regards herself as the only competitor for the acquisition of the Carolines," the United States pressed on with its effort, offering Spain $1 million for the island and "cable-landing rights in other Spanish territory" (an offer which, in turn, provoked an even stronger German denunciation of the American "policy of seeking islands all over the world for coaling stations").

What happened next is most revealing. Declining the American offer, Spain made an even more dramatic counterproposal—the cession of *all* the Carolines and *all* the Marianas in exchange for open door status for Spain in Cuba and Puerto Rico. In so doing, Spain appeared to be playing directly into the hands of the Reid-Frye-Davis group (and some of the American military) who had favored total American control in those islands all along. (Indeed, Reid and Frye implied at one juncture a hope that Spain would break off peace negotiations, giving America an excuse to take the islands.) These three commissioners gave their enthusiastic endorsement to the project and asked for permission to negotiate along the lines of the Spanish proposal (though perhaps with a time limit on the open door for Spain). But McKinley and Hay refused to pay such a price for something they neither needed nor desired. Seeking only individual cable and coaling stations for limited purposes, they were in no way disposed to exercise indiscriminate sovereignty over numerous, widely dispersed islands; to plant the Stars and Stripes on every ocean-bound rock and pebble they could get. Hay rejected the Spanish offer out-of-hand by return cable on December 4, and there the matter died. . . .

Thus the peace negotiations with Spain, initiated in September within the conscious framework of the Chinese question, concluded three months later on an identical note. Article IV of the treaty made clear the intimacy that bound Philippine and China policy: McKinley would keep his earlier promise to accord the open door in the Philippines, provided the United States received reciprocal treatment elsewhere in the orient. In actuality, this American open door was limited in time and scope, and it later vanished in the midst of emerging American economic aspirations in the Philippines themselves. But for the moment administration spokesmen regarded the proviso as *key* to future American policy in the Far East. Assistant Secretary of State A. A. Adee, that permanent fixture in the Department, stated unequivocally that "the open door paragraph is the most important"; and Whitelaw Reid, the peace commission's most powerful figure, insisted the open door for the Philippines "enables Great Britain and the United States to preserve a common interest and present a common front in the enormous development in the Far East that must attend the awakening of the Chinese Colossus."

The final treaty arrangements on the Philippines were the outgrowth of an evolving set of circumstances dating back to 1895, when the combined impact of the American depression and the Sino-Japanese War offered both the need and the hope that China might become the great absorber of America's industrial surplus. Subsequent developments, culminating in the partitioning of late 1897 and early 1898, critically threatened the hope but in no way dissipated the need. They did, however, dictate the desirability of finding some vigorous means of safeguarding America's present and future commercial stake in the Chinese Empire. Fortunately, the Spanish-American War provided just such an opportunity, and the McKinley administration was quick to exploit it. The result was the effective thrust of American influence into the far Pacific. From Honolulu through Wake and Guam to Manila stretched a chain of potential coaling, cable, and naval stations to serve as America's avenue to Asia. Only the construction of an isthmian canal remained to complete the system.

The grand scheme was not imperial—in the narrow sense of the word. The insular possessions in the Pacific were not pieces of empire, per se, but stepping-stones and levers to be utilized upon a larger and more important stage—China. Paradoxically, American expansion was designed in part to serve an anti-imperial purpose of preventing the colonization of China and thus preserving her for open door market penetration: *the imperialism of anti-imperialism* ("neo-colonialism" in today's parlance). All this McKinley captured in his Presidential Message of December 5, 1898, when he declared that our "vast commerce . . . and the necessity of our staple production for Chinese uses" had made the United States a not "indifferent spectator of the extraordinary" partitioning in China's maritime provinces. Nevertheless, he continued, so long as "no discriminatory treatment of American . . . trade be found to exist . . . the need for our country becoming an actor in the scene" would be "obviated." But, he concluded, the fate of the open door would not be left to chance; it would be, he said, "my aim to subserve our large interests in that quarter by all means appropriate to the constant policy of our government." Quite obviously, the fruits of the Spanish-American War had enormously multiplied the "appropriate . . . means" available to American policy-makers and had completed the setting for America's illusory search after that holy commercial grail—the China market.

eight
the thrust of
the agricultural
majority

WILLIAM A. WILLIAMS

Although most careful scholars deny that it exists, the
"Wisconsin School of Diplomatic History" has become a
simple catchword to describe William A. Williams
(b. 1921) and many of his students who have emphasized
the "open door" or economic expansion as the impetus
of American foreign policy for decades. LaFeber and
McCormick are usually placed in that "school." Whether
he has his own intellectual "school" or not, Williams ranks
as one of the most thoughtful and provocative historians
of the twentieth century. He is now professor of history at
Oregon State University. In The Tragedy of American
Diplomacy *(1962),* American-Russian Relations, 1787–1947
(1952), and The Roots of the Modern American Empire
(1969), from which the following selection is taken,
Williams has provided grand and controversial syntheses.
This selection is particularly interesting because it contrasts
with Williams's thesis in The Tragedy *that commercial*
interests thrust the United States into imperialism.

The expansionist, imperial foreign policy adopted by the
United States at the end of the nineteenth century was
largely formulated in industrial terms by men who were
leaders and spokesmen of that part of the political economy.

Source: William A. Williams, *The Roots of the Modern American
Empire: A Study of the Growth and Shaping of Social
Consciousness in a Marketplace Society* (New York: Random
House, 1969), pp. 4–5, 408–09, 414–18, 425–28. Copyright ©
1969 by William Appleman Williams. Reprinted by permission of
Random House, Inc.

They were primarily concerned with obtaining markets for surplus manufactured goods and venture capital, and with acquiring reliable access to cheap raw materials needed by the American industrial system. That industrial orientation of American foreign policy became increasingly clear during the twentieth century as American leaders struggled to build and maintain an international system that would satisfy the interrelated economic, ideological, and security needs and desires of the United States as they defined those objectives.

When the policy was crystallized in the latter years of the 1890s, and to an increasing degree in subsequent decades, the dynamics of the policy-making process centered in a relatively small group of economic, political, and intellectual leaders who characterized American interests and needs in those industrial-financial terms. Part of that centralization of power and authority was due to the inherent nature of government, particularly in a social system as large and as geographically extended as American society. Part of it was explained by the additionally inside, quasi-secret, and administrative character of foreign policy decisions in any government. Neither the majority itself nor a legislative assembly can handle policy matters on a routine basis. In the underlying sense, however, it was the result of the consolidation and centralization that accompanied the maturation of modern industrial capitalism in the United States, and which provided the industrial-financial leaders with their power base.

All of those factors have led historians to emphasize the industrial nature of the policy, and to stress the role of the small group of top policy makers. And, because of their power, authority, and influence in the political economy, those men have enjoyed and exercised a significant degree of sustained, unchallenged initiative. They have, of course, been subjected to pressures from various organized interest groups; and they have encountered resistance from other branches of the government, and from occasional upwellings of public feeling and opinion. Those forces have caused delays and shifts of emphasis in implementing the broad policy adopted at the turn of the century, but they have not produced major changes in the nature of the policy or a serious weakening of the power wielded by the leadership elite. In a great majority of instances, moreover, the more general opposition to one or another aspect of the policy developed around a dissident faction of the leaders. Such was the case, for example, in connection with the defeat of President Woodrow Wilson's effort to establish the League of Nations on the basis of America's policy and power.

Much later, the opposition to the Vietnam war manifested some characteristics which suggested that movement might develop as an exception to the general pattern of criticism of American foreign relations in the twentieth century. It is possible that the resolution of the war could involve, or lead into, a reevaluation and change of the imperial policy first codified during the 1890s. Even if that possibility becomes reality, however, it is apparent that the origins of the opposition to the war involved members of the policy-making elite as well as outside critics. But it would also be clear under such circumstances that widespread support had developed for a more far-reaching shift in outlook and policy.

Whatever may happen in connection with the Vietnam war, the historical evidence makes it apparent that precisely such an involvement of the majority of the adult population played a vital part in the evolution and adoption of the imperial policy at the end of the nineteenth century. American imperialism was not forced on the majority by a domestic elite, any more than it was imposed on the country by outside forces or foreign nations. That presents what appears to be a paradox. For, on the one hand, the majority of the American people from 1865 to 1900 was associated with the agricultural part of the political economy. Yet, on the other hand, the policy itself was formulated in industrial terms by leaders of that section of the system.

* * *

Historians cannot film the process of going to war as a physicist can record the flight of a man down a sand dune. Hence they cannot perfectly isolate the pivotal instant. But they can with confidence say that the decision occurred within a certain period. And with the McKinley Administration that moment came long before the President wrote his special war message of April 1898 to the Congress. The primary force producing the war against Spain was the marketplace-expansionist outlook generated by the agricultural majority of the country during the generation after the firing on Fort Sumter. That social consciousness involved an image of the world as a free capitalist marketplace in which personal and social freedoms were causally integrated with economic liberty and welfare, in which ideas and experience were merged as beliefs, and which promised ideal results from necessary actions.

The agricultural businessmen played a smaller, but by no means insignificant, part in the crucial definition of the war as an instrument of American expansion in Asia. But it was the metropolitans, rather than the agriculturalists, who explicitly formulated the war against Spain over Cuba as a war for the free marketplace in the Far East. The acceptance of that conception marked the shift in policy-making initiative away from the farm businessmen to metropolitan leaders. It was a decision of principle implemented with plans to fight a two-front war, and to hold some portion of Spain's Pacific empire as a springboard to the Asian marketplace.

* * *

McKinley moved slowly and carefully—"very deliberately," as Senator Lodge noted—on Cuba during the first two months after he took office. His typical very-close-to-the-buttoned-vest approach misled many people, including Lodge and other metropolitan expansionists, as well as the agriculturalists. For a time, the farm businessmen were themselves busy praising Secretary Wilson's vigorous effort to reopen old markets and penetrate new ones, agitating various expansionist measures such as a bill to add agricultural attachés to foreign legations, and adding their optimistic prognostications about the Asian market. Increasingly, however, they focused their attention and pressure on Cuba.

Senator Allen pushed his campaign to recognize the rebels so heatedly that the Washington *Post* warned that "a spark might drop in at any time and precipitate action." There were two sparks. One was Senator Morgan, who took over the battle with his resolution of April 1 to recognize "a condition of public war" in Cuba and extend "all the rights of belligerents" to the revolutionaries. The other was the increased ferocity and destructiveness of the rebels and the Spanish. That created intense emotion about the mistreatment of Americans and a heightened concern over the destruction of American economic interests.

Morgan argued powerfully that the only way to reverse the sharp and severe drop in exports to Cuba was to create an independent Cuba tied to the United States. Populists like Allen vigorously supported that analysis, but so did Republicans like Senator John Meelen Thurston of Nebraska and Senator Francis Emory Warren of Wyoming, Democrats like Representative John Sharp Williams of Mississippi, and Populist-Democrats like Curtis Harvey Castle of California. "Why should we not act?" Thurston argued. "We have with her, or had with her, a great and an advantageous trade relation. . . . Why should we not act? I will put it upon no other grounds than purely commercial grounds, if you please. . . . We have lost the advantage of the Cuban market."

Metropolitan expansionists like Lodge agreed with Thurston that the case for intervention could be made solely on economic grounds, and often presented that argument with great vigor. Many of that group shared the agricultural concern to spread freedom, moreover, although they often defined it more narrowly. Those men were opposed in the spring of 1897, however, by a stronger contingent of metropolitans who wanted peace in order to proceed with recovery at home and to pursue less dramatic economic expansion. They tried to blunt the influence of the hard-liners with petitions of their own. More than 300 of them from New Orleans and Charleston, as well as Boston, New York, and Philadelphia, for example, signaled their support of McKinley in May. It was a curious kind of support, however, that pointed toward their ultimate willingness to intervene. They wanted peace to end the great economic losses and to quiet the unrest generated by the war in Cuba, but they asked the President to use his power and authority to secure that result.

Most agriculturalists demanded far more direct intervention. Their resolution calling on McKinley to recognize the rebels as belligerents passed the Senate 41 to 14 on May 20, 1897; a demonstration of power that moved one group of peaceful expansionists to escalate their own efforts with a proposal to buy Cuba. McKinley would probably have gone along with that plan if it had ever become actionable (he kept it alive for months), but he was far too realistic to place much hope in that approach. The evidence is strong, indeed, that the President anticipated the ultimate necessity for intervention and war even as he came into office.

Assistant Secretary of State William R. Day, who was less militant than Secretary Sherman, felt that the President "probably" considered intervention from the outset. Another insider supported that estimate on the basis of his conversation with McKinley during the search for the right man to send as Minister to Spain. He quoted the President as saying that "if nothing could be done with Spain, he desired to show that he had spared no effort to avert trouble." Other indicators reinforce that analysis. Senator Eugene Hale of Maine told the Senate during the debate over belligerency for the rebels that the President was in full control of the situation; and the editors of *Farm, Field and Fireside* quickly spotted the important liaison between McKinley and Representative Hitt of Illinois, who had been a militant expansionist ever since his service with Blaine. And Senator Francis Emory Warren of Wyoming, who discussed the issue with McKinley in June, told a friend that the President was ready to act. . . .

The editors of *Farm, Field and Fireside* either had a good source of official information or the Administration was very closely attuned to the outlook of the agriculturalists. Probably both. They advised the President on July 3, in any event, that Woodford's instructions "should ask the virtual independence of Cuba, for the sake of the lives and safety of our own citizens, for the sake of commerce, for the sake of humanity." The heart of the Administration's dispatch dated July 15, 1897, stressed that "the extraordinary, because direct and not merely theoretical or sentimental, interest of the United States in the Cuban situation cannot be ignored, and if forced the issue must be met honestly and fearlessly, in conformity with our national life and character."

"Not only are our citizens largely concerned in the ownership of property and in the industrial and commercial ventures which have been set on foot in Cuba through our enterprising initiative and sustained by their capital, but the chronic condition of trouble and violent derangement in that island constantly causes disturbance in the social and political condition of our own people. It keeps up a continuous irritation within our own borders, injuriously affects the normal functions of business, and tends to delay the condition of prosperity to which this country is entitled. . . . Assuredly Spain can not expect the Government to sit idle, letting vast interests suffer, our political elements disturbed, and the country perpetually embroiled, while no progress is being made in the settlement of the Cuban problem. . . . You will not disguise the gravity of the situation, nor conceal the President's conviction that, should his present effort be fruitless, his duty to his countrymen will necessitate an early decision as to the course of action which the time and the transcendent emergency may demand."

Perhaps no official document of the era provides as clear a statement of the expansionist outlook that had been generated and shaped by the agricultural majority. Spain was held responsible for a prosperity to which the United States was "entitled." Misrule in Cuba, rather than the failure of the domestic political economy, was the actionable cause of America's difficulties. Equally important, the message established McKinley's deep concern with the increasingly aggressive demands for direct intervention by the militants headed by the agriculturalists and their spokesmen. That agitation was a product of the same conception of America's needs and objectives. The definition of the United States in terms of an expanding free marketplace and the frontier process had created a "transcendent emergency" that could only be resolved by a foreign power acting within that framework—or by war.

*   *   *

McKinley was unquestionably prepared to go to war, and to fight the war
with a two-front strategy, whenever he judged the agricultural militants on the
verge of splitting and taking control of the Republican party, and thereby
displacing the metropolis (and the party) as the dominant force in the political
economy. He was not, therefore, running an elaborate bluff, and most certainly
not scrambling desperately to maintain his control. It was one of the most
striking displays of presidential nerve and finesse in the nation's history.

The President counted on the agricultural war hawks, led by the Populists
and the Silverites, to push the die-hard metropolitan conservatives over the
line. That would save him, whatever the Spanish did, from having to split the
head of the party to avoid severing the head from the body. The militants
wasted no time in performing as anticipated. "I am the jingo of jingoes," cried
Senator Allen joyfully, as he saw the long campaign approaching victory.
With the help of Southern allies like Senators Butler, Call, and Morgan, the
United States was going to meet its responsibilities as Cuba's "elder brother"
and displace Great Britain as the monarch of the marketplace.

Allen's claim to a place in the vanguard of the agricultural spokesmen who
forced the issues cannot be denied, but he had much assistance. Even Simpson
["Sockless Jerry," nationally famous farm leader], who avowed a primary
concern for the condition of American society, bowed to the emergency and
voted for three new battleships. And the editors of Populist and silver papers
constantly agitated the issues, arguing that war would extend freedom and
exports, and concluding that, if it brought the remonetization of silver, it
"would not be an unmitigated evil."

But the Populists were in truth but the whitecaps on the ground swells
of agricultural expansionism. The more conservative farm businessmen had
been agitating overseas markets for more than a generation before the Populists
appeared. Indeed, the vast majority of Populists were erstwhile Democrats
and Republicans who had been part of that expansionist movement. Editor
E. S. Jones of the *Prairie Farmer* candidly acknowledged the economic stake
involved in the crisis. "Stripped of all questions of sentimentalism," the issue
was trade. Trade "of especial importance to farmers of this country. With
normal conditions prevailing, Cuba has been a large consumer of our
agricultural products, and should be a much larger consumer of them than
heretofore, with the establishment of peace and sound government." Those
conditions would create a "large and permanent demand." The political
spokesmen of the moderate and even conservative agricultural businessmen
argued just as powerfully for intervention.

Such a combination of fury and reason enlisted in behalf of freedom and
trade had the expected effect on the metropolis. The "head of a leading stock
Exchange house" was reported on March 9 as concerned lest the "internal
dissension" over Cuba delay and weaken "the extension of commerce with the
rest of the world." Stuyvesant Fish of the Illinois Central verified the same
shift of opinion. And on March 15 Cleveland Dodge told Secretary of War

Russell A. Alger that the businessmen were deeply concerned about the
continuing discord. "They are willing to go to any extreme to avoid it." Alger's
reply provided a good insight into Administration thinking on the issue. He
emphasized the economic disruption, and made it clear that he was ready to
"meet this question and settle it forever now."

Such evidence makes it clear that the financial and industrial laggards were
moving toward war *before* Senator Redfield Proctor delivered his famous
speech of March 17, which has so often been credited with turning the tide in
the metropolis. Just as Proctor had been an expansionist toward Cuba for many
years, so metropolitan attitudes had never been wholly pacific. The legislature
of the State of New York, for example, appealed to McKinley on January 31
to secure peace "by whatever means necessity may require." A large delegation
of New Yorkers then discussed the problem with the President early in
February, stressing the need to settle the issue before May or June in order to
plant and harvest the sugar crop. The continuing uncertainty, steadily increased
and made more threatening by the agricultural campaign for war with silver,
would have completed the metropolitan conversion to war even if Senator
Proctor had never spoken.

The President's messages to the metropolis were far more important than
Proctor's words. Personal emissaries, associates acting as campaigners, and
political appointees serving as errand boys usually accomplish more than
speeches in such circumstances. McKinley used all those approaches after
the White House conference on appropriations—and had no doubt done so
before. Once the metropolitan tide began to flood, moreover, it crashed upon
the White House with almost as much force as the agricultural surf. The same
militant cry came from New York, Boston, and Philadelphia: "With force
if we must."

A sizable group of Republican leaders began during the last week of March
to demand an immediate declaration of war. They feared the Populist and
Democratic agriculturalists would exploit the consensus for war to their
immediate and long-range advantage. McKinley held them off with a firm
assertion of his will cloaked in the folds of the constitutional division of powers
(and a telegram campaign for peace very probably organized by Hanna) until he
completed his preparations and offered Spain one last chance to surrender
without war. He gave the Congress its head on April 11, but acted as
Commander in Chief even before the representatives and senators could
settle their differences and pass a war resolution. As a result, the declaration
of war voted on April 25 had to be dated April 21 to cover the naval action
initiated by the United States on April 22, 1898.

The editors of the *Southern Mercury,* failing to distinguish between McKinley
and Cleveland, "never believed that there would be any war." When it came,
therefore, they largely explained it as a diversion engineered by the metropolis.
But one Texas Populist could not accept either the faulty analysis or the evasion
of responsibility. His sharp rebuke was far closer to the truth about the
immediate and historical role of the agricultural businessmen. "We as Populists
ought to be candid," J. S. Woods admonished the editors. "Since 1896 all the

leading Populists in National, State, and county conventions have declared in some way favorable towards freeing Cuba."

"All this talk about imperialism," he continued, "is but the old howl of the Federalists when they arrayed themselves against Mr. Jefferson for securing to this Nation the Louisiana purchase and the opening of the mouth of the Mississippi river for the benefit of trade and commerce. . . . Let the southern and especially Texas Populists stand firm for a policy which will put us in touch with five hundred millions of Asiatic consumers, where the people of Texas, the South, and the West, can sell all of their surplus products, cotton goods, wheat, flour, iron and beef; then we will be free from the power of Lombard Street and England will no longer be able to dictate and control the prices of productive labor in the South. Give us an exchange market in Cuba, Porto Rico, the Philippines, Caroline Islands, and in China and Japan. . . . Let no Populist be led astray by the scare-crow of words manufactured by such men as Cleveland. . . . Free commerce is what we want. . . . The capture of these islands . . . means universal free trade for this nation and an expansion of our National thought, commerce and trade, and it further means death to the cruel and dishonest methods of gain heretofore imposed upon us in the South and West by the bondholders of Europe and New England."

Other agriculturalists in the West and Northwest echoed his analysis. "The war is upon us," commented the editor of the *Western Rural,* and then went to the point. "It is of our own making and was inspired by the principles of humanity . . . the spirit of liberty and progress." Once the war for a free marketplace in Cuba had come, the editors of the *Rural New Yorker* turned to Asia and explained why nations were edging toward war in China. "Once make them believe that they should have two suits of clothes, and you create a clothing trade. . . . American manufacturers are, or ought to be, able to hold their own in foreign trade. American farmers may expect a constantly increasing foreign demand for food and, indirectly, the opening up and civilizing of Africa and China will increase this demand."

The agricultural majority had played the primary causal role in generating the ideas, emotions, and policy that produced the war against Spain, and struggled persistently to define the war as one to extend the freedoms of a marketplace society as well as to expand exports. The farm businessmen subsequently supported the policy developed by the metropolis from their outlook and ideas. And for that reason the war for the free marketplace led on to a marketplace empire.

nine
the foreign policy elite and international influence

ERNEST R. MAY

When American Imperialism: A Speculative Essay *appeared
in 1968, Ernest R. May (b. 1928) had already written*
The World War and American Isolation, 1914–1917
(1959) and Imperial Democracy *(1961). They revealed
multiarchival research and an approach that found
American leaders often groping for a foreign policy, seldom
seeking international power, and influenced more by
events abroad than by careful planning in Washington.
May, professor of history at Harvard University, extends
his thinking in* American Imperialism *to "speculate" that the
foreign policy elite, consisting of a small number of people
knowledgeable and concerned about foreign relations
issues, borrowed ideas from imperial Europeans. May also
attempts a synthesis of other interpretations by delineating
a number of motives at work. The question for him is
the political process.*

In 1898–99 the United States suddenly became a colonial
power. It annexed the Hawaiian Islands. Humbling Spain in
a short war, it took Puerto Rico and the Philippines. In
quick sequence it also acquired Guam and part of Samoa

Source: Ernest R. May, *American Imperialism: A Speculative Essay*
(New York: Atheneum Publishers, 1968), pp. 3–16, 44–49,
54–55, 72, 226, 228–30. Copyright © 1967, 1968 by Ernest R. May
Reprinted by permission of Atheneum Publishers.

and, if the Danish Rigsdag had consented, would have bought the Virgin Islands. In an eighteen-month period it became master of empires in the Caribbean and the Pacific.

Viewing America's tradition as anticolonial, historians have found these events puzzling. The legislative resolution for war with Spain seemingly expressed this tradition. Calling for independence for Spain's Cuban colony, Congress disclaimed "any disposition or intention to exercise sovereignty, jurisdiction, or control over" Cuba. That the same body should have ended the war by annexing Puerto Rico and Spanish islands in the Pacific appears a paradox, and many historians see 1898–99 as, in Samuel Flagg Bemis' phrase, a "great aberration."

To be sure, Americans of the time were hustled along by events. The first battle of the war took place not in Cuba but in Spain's more distant Philippine colony. A spectacular success, in which Admiral Dewey's squadron overcame all opposition without losing a single ship or life, it surprised many Americans into their first awareness that the Philippine Islands existed and that Spain owned them. Soon, however, following reports that Dewey's victory had shaken Spain's control, American troops sailed to seize the colonial capital, Manila. On the ground that these troops would need a support base in mid-Pacific, Congress annexed the Hawaiian Islands. By war's end, therefore, the United States already had one Pacific colony, and debate centered on whether to acquire another in the Philippines.

Both Americans and Europeans assumed that the United States could dispose of the Philippines as it chose. Seeming alternatives included handing the islands back to Spain, arranging for transfer to a European power, insisting on independence, or annexing. Most Americans saw the first alternative as giving up a hard-won prize and, moreover, returning the Filipinos to virtual slavery; the second as throwing an apple of discord among European states, perhaps even leading to general war; and the third, given the low level of Philippine development, as infeasible. Annexation appeared the least unattractive course.

American politicians could reason so, however, only by assuming that annexation would not cost votes at home. The historical puzzle rises from the fact that politicians then in power apparently did not expect to pay a price at the polls. Why not? With anticolonialism as strong as the Congressional war resolution suggests, how could politicians conclude that a colonialist policy could safely be pursued?

In *Expansionists of 1898* Julius W. Pratt offers part of an answer. He shows that, after Dewey's victory, religious journals changed tone. The Baptist *Standard,* the Presbyterian *Interior* and *Evangelist,* the Congregationalist *Advance,* and the *Catholic World* all spoke of rule over the Philippines as America's Christian duty. Methodist, Episcopalian, and Campbellite organs said the same. Only Quaker and Unitarian papers stood unitedly in opposition.

Pratt also shows the business press following a similar pattern. Having in the past either opposed or said nothing about acquisition of new territory, business journals now talked of the advantages of expansion. . . .

Before finally making up his mind, President McKinley toured the Midwest. Standing before large audiences, he delivered equivocal speeches. Some lines hinted at a decision to annex the Philippines; other lines hinted the opposite. His staff took notes on the relative levels of applause and reported that proannexation words drew louder handclaps. Other public figures presumably had similar experiences. Politicians thus had before them persuasive evidence of a dramatic swing in public opinion.

Such evidence explains their behavior partly but not entirely. In the past they had had plenty of evidence of antiexpansionist feeling. Though knowing in 1890 that minor tariff changes could encourage Canadians to seek annexation, congressmen found so little public enthusiasm that they failed to enact the changes. When voting the war resolution, they evidently felt that the people would not want Cuba. One might suppose that politicians would have anticipated the public's recovery from a momentary fancy for Pacific colonies and its repudiation of the officeholders who had pandered to such a perversion. That politicians showed no such fear must mean that they had some basis for believing the whim would endure. They must have seen some impulse stronger than momentary excitement over victories in far-off places. What can it have been? What conditions existed conducive to a lasting popular movement in favor of imperialism?

This question has challenged historians. Setting aside versions that stress Providence, the westward trend, or inherent tendencies in capitalism, one can single out four major efforts to answer it. Each emphasizes a different factor.

Frederick Merk, the preeminent historian of American expansion in the 1840s, argues that a long-lived Manifest Destiny tradition offset the anticolonial tradition. In *Manifest Destiny and Mission in American History* he describes two schools of thought existing at the time of the Mexican War. One, he says, favored the acquisition of territory in order to increase the nation's wealth and power. The other laid more stress on America's mission as the exemplar of democracy and individual liberty. After the victories of Taylor and Scott, men in the first school favored taking all or most of Mexico. Those in the second school wanted only sparsely inhabited tracts which settlers could easily turn into other Kentuckys and Ohios. In an epilogue on the 1890s Merk suggests that the ideas of the first, or Manifest Destiny, school reappeared later as imperialism, while the idea of Mission persisted as anti-imperialism. The two traditions had had equal hardihood, and the circumstances of 1898–99 gave the expansionist tradition an edge.

Explaining the actions of McKinley and other politicians would be an awareness of the expansionist tradition and an assumption that the balance had tipped toward it and away from the tradition of Mission. For parallels one might think of politicians concluding in 1913 that the protectionist tradition had lost out to the free-trade tradition or, in 1964, that states' rights had lost out to civil rights. In Merk's view the Manifest Destiny tradition provides the key to understanding what happened in 1898–99.

Julius Pratt emphasizes Social Darwinism. In *Expansionists of 1898* and elsewhere Pratt describes the expansionism of the 1890s as having a different rationale from that of pre-Civil War days. It took from Herbert Spencer and other writers the idea of an endless struggle testing each nation's fitness to survive. On this premise the United States had to seize whatever share of the earth it could, for not to do so would give advantages to rivals and in the long run would lead to defeat, decay, and decline. Expansion presented itself not as an open choice but as a necessity dictated by stern scientific law.

The premise already had wide acceptance. Dealing with domestic economic and social issues, writers and clergymen commonly invoked such formulae as "struggle for survival" and "survival of the fittest." At an early point some Americans progressed to conclusions about how the United States should behave internationally. Pointing to the navy's shift from sail to steam, they argued that the United States would stand at a dangerous disadvantage without coaling stations in distant seas. The Spanish War then created opportunities for acquiring such stations, far out in the Pacific as well as in the Caribbean. It also placed in America's grasp territories which, if not seized, could go to potential rivals. And it offered a seeming chance for Protestant Christianity (also a species, by Social Darwinist canons) to score a gain in its struggle for survival against Catholicism and heathenism. In Pratt's view these Social Darwinist theses captured American public opinion. The anticolonial tradition would not have intimidated politicians, because they would have expected these new ideas to dominate future public thinking about foreign policy.

In *The New Empire,* a more recent book than either Merk's or Pratt's, Walter LaFeber stresses economic forces. Like Pratt, he regards post-Civil War expansionism as different from that of the prewar era, but different because businessmen now captained the country and set their sights on markets rather than land. Whether manufacturers, merchants, or investors, they feared lest America's multiplying factories produce more than Americans could buy. As European states laid on protective tariffs, their thoughts turned to colonies and spheres of influence. Politicians behaved as they did in the 1890s, LaFeber suggests, because they put the interests of business ahead of all else, assumed the electorate would do the same, judged colonial expansion to serve business, and counted on the public's coming to the same conclusion and endorsing their actions.

A fourth major interpretation of the period, that of Richard Hofstadter, describes expansionism as merely one manifestation of a widespread "psychic crisis." The rise of bigger, more powerful, and more bureaucratized business organizations produced protest in strikes such as those at Homestead and Pullman and political movements such as those of the Populists and Bryanite Democrats. These forms of protest failed. Meanwhile, with such savants as Frederick Jackson Turner warning that the free land frontier no longer existed to drain off the discontented, members of the urban middle class took alarm not only at the growth of big business but at the radicalism of the protesters. For Americans in all these groups, Hofstadter argues, war with Spain and annexation of distant islands represented an escape from reality—madcap behavior comparable to that of disturbed adolescents. Politicians presumably counted on the public's remaining in this state of mind and applauding the acquisition of new frontiers rather than swinging back to disapproval of expansion.

The interpretations of Merk, Pratt, LaFeber, and Hofstadter can be reconciled. One could picture LaFeber's businessmen as borrowers of the

Manifest Destiny tradition, differing from expansionists of the 1840s in questing for consumers rather than resources and quoting Herbert Spencer instead of the Book of Genesis, and one could explain their success in the 1890s as due to the "psychic crisis." But even such a blend of interpretations leaves two questions unanswered.

The first has to do with process. Merk does not say how the Manifest Destiny tradition came temporarily to outbalance the tradition of Mission. Pratt does not show how the Social Darwinist prescription won acceptance. LaFeber fails to explain how businessmen came to see expansion as in their interest. Hofstadter offers no reason why men caught in a "psychic crisis" concluded that Pacific islands would be good things to have. No one charts the phases through which the individuals making up the public might have passed as they changed their convictions about colonies.

The second open question has to do with timing. Why did the change take place when it did?

Through the 1870s and 1880s the tradition of Mission, as Merk interprets it, appeared to hold the field. The influence of Social Darwinism did not extend to thought about foreign policy, and businessmen gave few signs of seeing colonial expansion as an answer to overproduction. At the end of the eighties, reports that Germany was about to take over Samoa produced some discussion of America's interest in the islands. Though no one spoke as a full-fledged expansionist, not everyone adopted the doctrinaire view that the United States could not consider taking part of the archipelago.

When Americans in Hawaii overthrew the native ruler in 1893 and appealed for annexation by the United States, politicians and newspaper reporters detected a surprising degree of public support for such a step. Some historians have concluded that if President Grover Cleveland had been of a mind to acquire the islands, he could have carried Congress and the country with him. Thus, despite the public's show of disinterest in annexing Canada and despite the language in Congress' 1898 war resolution, some shift away from anticolonialism could be observed even before Dewey's victory and its sequel. Circumstances created by the war will not account entirely for the estimates of public opinion formed by McKinley and other politicians. One has to ask why an apparent change in public attitudes should have set in around the beginning of the nineties.

Merk does not deal with this question. Pratt does so only indirectly. Describing books and essays by Josiah Strong, John Fiske, John W. Burgess, Alfred Thayer Mahan, and Henry Cabot Lodge that appeared after 1885, he implies that these writings had continuing and growing influence. LaFeber has at least a partial answer. According to his reconstruction, the idea of colonial expansion as a partial solution to overproduction gained ground after 1879, when European states began putting up protective tariffs, and became much more attractive when the domestic market suddenly shrank in the panic of 1893. Hofstadter responds to the question by saying, in effect, that the turn to expansionism originated in the "psychic crisis" and that, since the "psychic crisis" occurred in the 1890s, it could only have come at that time.

But the timing of American imperialism has an aspect that neither LaFeber nor Hofstadter adequately explains. Change occurred after 1898 as well as before. After annexing the Philippines and negotiating treaties for acquisition of part of Samoa and all of the Danish West Indies, McKinley stood for reelection. He won by a larger margin than in 1896, in a contest characterized by his Democratic opponent as a referendum on imperialism. After his assassination in 1901 the presidency went to Vice President Theodore Roosevelt, who had been an ardent champion of colonial expansion. Yet the United States did not continue a career as an imperial power.

Not only did the American government make no efforts after 1900 to acquire new islands in the Caribbean or Pacific, it deliberately spurned opportunities to do so. Theodore Roosevelt rebuffed Haitians and Dominicans who dropped proannexation hints, and during nearly eight years as President he acquired only one piece of real estate—the ten-mile-wide Canal Zone in Panama. Though one may cite the Platt Amendment, as applied to Cuba, the acquisition of the Canal Zone, and the Roosevelt Corollary to the Monroe Doctrine as evidence that the United States still had a mild case of imperialism, the nation's expansion as a colonial power effectively came to an end as of 1899 or 1900.

After that date, moreover, politicians reverted to the working assumption they had employed before 1898. McKinley and Roosevelt took it for granted that public opinion would not approve keeping Cuba as a colony. They judged that acquisition of a leasehold in China or annexation of Haiti, Santo Domingo, or a portion of Central America would be unpopular. And no evidence contradicted these judgments. After 1900 scarcely a congressman or newspaper editor raised his voice in favor of further colonial extension. Imperialism as a current in American public opinion appeared to be dead.

None of the theories concerning the rise of the imperialist movement satisfactorily explains its sudden demise. While Merk may be right that, over the long term, Mission had more power than Manifest Destiny, such a hypothesis does not in itself explain why, in this instance, Manifest Destiny enjoyed such short-lived ascendancy. Social Darwinism, the factor stressed by Pratt, had as much currency in 1902 as in 1898, yet seemed not to work the same effect on thought about foreign policy. LaFeber's businessmen had the same standing as before and regarded overproduction with only a little, if any, less concern. No apparent economic factor would account for their having different feelings about colonies. If a "psychic crisis" actuated imperialism, then it must have been literally a crisis, followed by quick recovery.

None of these comments depreciates the work of Merk, Pratt, LaFeber, and Hofstadter: all historians leave some questions unanswered. Nor does the present essay pretend to prove any of the four wrong. To the factors they have stressed, it adds a fifth—the impact on Americans of English and European examples. It does not, however, assert that this influence dominated. As much synthesis as reinterpretation, this study endeavors to portray the public that would have had opinion about expansion and to indicate how tradition, Social Darwinism, market hunger, psychological turmoil, *and* awareness of foreign

fashions combined to cause a shift away from the anticolonial tradition
at about the beginning of the 1890s, an upsurge of genuine imperialism in
1898–99, and then an abrupt return to the earlier faith.

* * *

Owing to historic factors, the pretensions of its old families, and an
essentially mercantile economy, Boston and its suburbs had many residents
equipped by education, attainments, and connections to lead opinion on the
colonial issue.

Thomas Jefferson Coolidge typified this comparatively large foreign policy
elite. His autobiography and collected private papers tell us a good deal
about him, and from recent historical studies by Barbara Solomon, Arthur
Mann, and Geoffrey Blodgett we know that he had little to do with molding
public opinion on domestic issues. He thus exemplifies the specialized opinion
leader—a prototype member of what today we call the foreign policy
establishment.

Born in 1831 into a securely rich family, Coolidge took his primary and
secondary schooling in England and Switzerland and then attended Harvard.
Entering business, he became, by his late forties, president of the Merchants
Bank of Boston and a heavy investor in railroads, serving at one time as
president of the Santa Fe and, at another, as a director of the Chicago,
Burlington, and Quincy. Owning land in the center of Birmingham, Alabama,
he built stores that prospered from Birmingham's sudden boom. Not all his
gambles succeeded. An electric light plant in Topeka, Kansas, for example,
resulted in a loss. Its optimistic manager wrote, "A coupon cutter and a
Dividend payer, are the next inventions I look for in connection with this
versatile agent"; but he proved unable to deliver. Nevertheless, in association
with other financiers, Coolidge made many a dollar from well-timed purchases
and sales of bonds, stocks, lands, and buildings.

Owning most if not all the characteristics of a robber baron, Coolidge could
write the following record of a conversation with a rental agent: "He said
the woman who occupies the Anderson property cannot pay rent. I directed
him to turn her out and I would make the house into two tenements which
could be rented." On another occasion Coolidge advised a friend not to accept
a certain mortgage, cautioning, "It is very hard to collect either interest or
capital from the Church without putting your hand in your pocket to help
the good cause." Property in Birmingham attracted him because of "the endless
supply of black labor." When profit beckoned he speculated in any
commodity, including opium.

In domestic politics Coolidge also showed the temper of a robber baron.
One of his letters gave marching orders for the senators and representatives
from Nebraska who "are obeying the C.B.&Q." As the largest shareholder in
the Amoskeag Cotton Mills, he maintained an agent in Manchester, New
Hampshire, who labored to prevent "radical legislation." He himself spent
time in Washington lobbying for protective duties on textiles.

Yet the press quoted him, and politicians sought his views and estimates of public feeling only on foreign policy problems, and not even on cotton tariffs. Reporters for Boston papers and for the Springfield *Republican* sought him out during a crisis with Chile of 1891–92, a crisis with Britain four years later over the Venezuela-Guiana boundary, the blowing up of the *Maine*, war with Spain, and the question of whether or not to annex the Philippines. James G. Blaine, when Secretary of State for Benjamin Harrison, expressed interest in Coolidge's views on possible complications with Germany in the Pacific. Both of Massachusetts' senators solicited his reactions to their positions on other foreign policy issues, including colonial expansion. Journalists in his home community and politicians in Washington evidently attached special weight to Coolidge's views on foreign policy.

He possessed unusually wide knowledge of the world. Fluent in French and familiar with English and European culture from his early education, he subsequently traveled much, not only in Europe but also in out-of-the-way places, such as Alexandria and Port au Prince, which most Americans discovered only as datelines on crisis reports. In 1889 he served as a delegate to the first Pan American Conference. In 1892–93 he spent a year as United States Minister to France.

Partly as a result of his travels and his diplomatic experience, Coolidge knew leading figures abroad. He could speak familiarly of such English and French statesmen as Joseph Chamberlain, Arthur Balfour, Jules Ferry, and Gabriel Hanotaux. He could name for President Harrison the men in England who would hold the keys to an international agreement on bimetallism and advise Massachusetts' Senator George F. Hoar on whether a proposed emissary would have the proper entree to this group. Interested citizens and politicians probably looked to Coolidge as an opinion leader primarily because of his firsthand knowledge of foreign places and inside knowledge of foreign politics.

Coolidge's near contemporary, William C. Endicott, possessed comparable qualifications. A noted lawyer, onetime judge and holder of large and profitable railroad investments, he had been Secretary of War during Cleveland's first administration, and his daughter had married the celebrated English politician, Joseph Chamberlain. When in England, he met the great and near great, and through his daughter and her friends received inside news of British and European political developments. Like Coolidge, Endicott could set Washington straight as to who pulled strings in London, and both politicians and newspapermen looked upon him as an authority on foreign affairs.

Richard Olney did not have quite the background of Coolidge or Endicott. Though of an old family, he came from western Massachusetts, and he had a bachelor's degree from Brown rather than Harvard. A hardworking, somewhat solitary railroad lawyer, he traveled little and gained none of Coolidge's or Endicott's firsthand knowledge of foreign statesmen. Before the 1890s he could have qualified as a leader of opinion on certain domestic issues, but hardly on foreign policy. In Cleveland's second administration, however, Olney served first as Attorney General and then, for two years, as Secretary of State. Coupled with his professional distinction, this experience caused him too to become a target of reporters' questions and of inquiring letters from politicians.

The circle of foreign policy leaders in Boston probably included also President

Charles W. Eliot of Harvard. Of a high-caste family and equipped, of course, with a Harvard diploma, Eliot had lived in France and Germany and made many trips to England. He could claim friendship with Bryce and other eminent Englishmen, and he could speak with authority not only on European education but also on English government and the English colonial system.

* * *

Men such as Coolidge, Endicott, and Eliot had a sense of the nation's complex traditions. Most had some acquaintance with Darwinian ideas as applied to current problems. . . . As capitalists or corporation lawyers, Coolidge, Endicott, Olney, and Elder watched out not only for the interests of their own companies or clients but for the general welfare of American business. And some at least participated in what Hofstadter calls the "psychic crisis." In 1891, when workingmen and agrarians had only begun to agitate, Coolidge prophesied darkly, "communism will in time destroy not only the stock capital, but the bonds which are . . . the accumulation of labor." The distinction between these men and others sensitive to tradition, imbued with Darwinism, concerned about business, or irrationally anxious about the future, lay chiefly in their having special familiarity with, even inside knowledge of, European politics.

* * *

By focusing on leaders of opinion we do not necessarily commit ourselves to the proposition that only an elite counted. If, however, only a relatively small public concerned itself with foreign policy issues, its members would have known the special qualifications of certain individuals, and these individuals would have functioned in some sense as opinion leaders. By examining the influences working on these leaders we can perhaps come somewhat closer to understanding why opinion within the foreign policy public changed during the 1890s.

* * *

Primarily the object of this essay is to set forth a synthetic interpretation of a single episode. Trying to take account of the easily forgotten fact that public opinion is seldom if ever opinion among more than an interested minority of the electorate, it has emphasized the small group of opinion leaders that gave this minority some guidance and, perhaps more importantly, provided political leaders with evidence as to how the interested public might bend.

Though these opinion leaders seemed for an interval not to be directing or representing the public, that interval was short. Most of the time the men whom we have described as members of the foreign policy establishment served as the voices of effective opinion, and their expressed views underwent changes. Through the 1870s and 1880s they opposed America's acquiring colonies. By 1893 they had adopted a different outlook and, by and large, approved of annexing Hawaii. Only from the outbreak of the Spanish war in

1898 to some point in 1900 or 1901 did they not either concur or divide along clear lines corresponding to party lines. After 1901 they agreed once again that the United States did not need and should not want colonial possessions. . . .

International fashions in thought and events on the world scene could have had a decisive influence on men of the establishment. Not that they attached more importance to keeping step with Europeans than to preserving tradition, furthering trade, obeying scientific laws, or preventing domestic upheaval. Quite the contrary. But knowledge of foreign thought affected their ideas about America's world mission and their understanding of Social Darwinism. Observation of foreign experience suggested to them alternative methods of promoting national prosperity and dealing with social discontent. Above all, the foreign scene provided models for imitation (reference groups and reference idols, in social science jargon). The well-traveled and well-read American could select a position on the colonial issue by identifying it with, on the one hand, [John] Bright, [William E.] Gladstone, [John] Morley, and [Eugen] Richter or, on the other, [Archibald Philip] Rosebery, [Neville] Chamberlain, [Jules François] Ferry, [Otto von] Bismarck, or Wilhelm II. Neither the American past nor an assessment of American economic needs nor Social Darwinism nor the domestic political scene offered such guidance.

Men of the establishment belonged both to their own country and to a larger Atlantic community. Ordinarily they defined opinion for an interested public, most of whom had less familiarity with currents abroad. Probably this fact explains in part why, when the establishment ceased to be coherent and leadership dispersed, apparent public opinion on colonies became so simplistic and emotional. It may also explain why, when the interested public appeared to be expanding, many politicians took an antiestablishment tack: they realized that a gulf separated the citizen of the Atlantic community from the citizen whose outlook comprehended only his county or state. Currents running within the larger community help to account for American public opinion not so much because they influenced a large number of Americans as because they influenced the few who set styles within a normally small foreign policy public.

As stated in the beginning, this essay does not dispute what other historians have said. On the contrary, it seeks to draw together previous interpretations by means of hypotheses about late nineteenth-century public opinion, its manifestations, and the play within it of tradition, economic interest, Social Darwinism, and psychological malaise, together with awareness of ideas and events abroad. I hope others will advance alternative hypotheses, for my aim is not to close debate but rather to reopen it by prompting new questions about this and other episodes. In the literal meaning of the term, this work is an essay.

part two
anti-imperialism: the rejected alternative

ten
the anti-imperialist as mugwump: successes and failures

ROBERT L. BEISNER

Robert L. Beisner (b. 1936) of American University has joined Fred H. Harrington and E. Berkeley Tompkins, among others, in researching the anti-imperialists and discovering their diversity. Beisner has concentrated on the independent, reform-conscious "mugwumps" who organized the Anti-Imperialist League, but who failed to derail America's imperialist thrust. He provides a balance sheet on their performance as dissenters in Twelve against War: The Anti-Imperialists, 1898–1900 *(1968), which won the Allan Nevins Prize from the Society of American Historians. Beisner's treatment allows the reader to compare the anti-imperialists with the imperialists in motives, ideas, political acumen, influence, and results. Professor Beisner has also written articles for scholarly journals, including* "1898 and 1968: The Anti-Imperialists and the Doves," *which appeared in the* Political Science Quarterly *in 1970.*

A few days after the United States Senate ratified the Treaty of Paris, the old abolitionist Thomas Wentworth Higginson attended a local meeting of the Anti-Imperialist League

Source: Robert L. Beisner, *Twelve Against Empire: The Anti-Imperialists, 1898–1900* (New York: McGraw-Hill, 1971), pp. 5, 7–14, 17, 216–20, 226–28, 230–39. Copyright © 1968 by Robert L. Beisner. Used with permission of McGraw-Hill Book Company.

and returned home to note in his diary that it had "seemed like an old Mugwump gathering." Higginson's observation was both accurate and obvious, for a striking parallel did exist between mugwumpery and anti-imperialism. In June, 1884, for instance, when Boston newspapers had printed a "Call" publicizing the unwillingness of a number of local Brahmins to support James G. Blaine, the Republican candidate for President, the signers included Higginson, Charles R. Codman, William Endicott, Jr., Moorfield Storey, Edward Atkinson, Charles W. Eliot, Charles Francis Adams, Jr., Winslow Warren, William Lloyd Garrison, Jr., Erving Winslow, Gamaliel Bradford, and Thomas Bailey Aldrich—all known as "mugwumps" in 1884 and later to be among the anti-imperialists of the 1890s. In fact, a large proportion of the most active anti-imperialists were political independents, "mugwumps" in the strictest sense. They had spent a good part of their mature lives bolting from one party to another or systematically proclaiming their independence of any party. They were political mavericks who saw no value in party loyalty as such. Regardless of its origins or onetime virtues, they believed a party was no more than what its current principles, policies, and leaders made it. . . .

Mugwumps also looked upon themselves as heralds of reform, at liberty to use their uncommitted votes to force reform upon the existing political parties or, if reforms were resisted, to threaten the parties with destruction. If need be, the mugwumps stood ready to create a new political grouping of high moral commitment, just as they had done when they helped found the Republican Party in the 1850s. As Thomas Wentworth Higginson explained to a Boston audience in 1873, party organizations "are truly prosperous only in advancing that idea which gave them birth," and, just as the Democrats had long outlived their Jeffersonian beginnings, so now the Republicans were losing sight of their founding principles, thus proving once again that "reform must be accomplished first by the free lances. . . ." The mugwump was seldom deflected from his purpose by the knowledge that as a "free lance" reformer he would often be in the minority or by the certainty that at times he would be derided and persecuted in the pursuit of his vision. Political virtue was its own reward, and, in any case, the truth would ultimately prevail and he would be vindicated. The mugwumps of 1898 knew they were right. . . .

Above all, the mugwump thought that his first duty in politics was to be true to himself. He did not look to successful results for justification of his position. He believed that as long as he pursued the right as he saw it, no other defense of his conduct was necessary. Neither party nor country could hope to receive his loyalty if it afforded him no moral justification for extending it. "A man's first duty," wrote Mark Twain to William Dean Howells in 1884, "is to his own conscience & honor—the party & the country come second to that, & never first . . . the only necessary thing to do, as I understand it, is that a man shall keep *himself* clean, (by withholding his vote for an improper man), even though the party & the country go to destruction in consequence."

Being a mugwump involved more than voting according to certain moral principles. It is also involved belonging to what Richard Hofstadter has called a "mugwump culture." In their own eyes mugwumps were the representatives of the "highest intelligence and the best culture of the country," the people who possessed "moral weight" or "solid character." More often than not, the mugwump saw himself as a person with an indisputable right to lead his country. This complacence reflected the fact that most leading mugwumps were men of substantial backgrounds, comfortable circumstances, and long-established Anglo-Saxon stock, in many cases the direct descendants of seventeenth-century New Englanders. They had received excellent educations, often at Harvard. Some of them lived on independent and inherited incomes. A recent study of the mugwumps in the state of New York who led the campaign for Cleveland in 1884 shows that out of a sample list of 396 mugwump names, 100 (or 25 per cent) could be found in the *Social Register*. Included in the sample were 101 lawyers, 97 businessmen, 57 financiers, 27 journalists, 25 physicians, 25 teachers, 22 white-collar workers, and 13 clergymen. It comes as no surprise to find that "only one labor leader and one farmer were found in the sample."

Although many of the New York mugwumps of 1884 were young men in their twenties and thirties, the leading mugwump anti-imperialists of the late 1890s, most of them New Englanders, were a much older group. Among them were Thomas Wentworth Higginson, who turned seventy-five in 1898; William Endicott, seventy-two; Charles Eliot Norton and Edward Atkinson, both seventy-one; James Burrill Angell, Charles Codman, and Carl Schurz, all sixty-nine; E. L. Godkin and Gamaliel Bradford, sixty-seven; Horace White and Charles W. Eliot, sixty-four; Charles Francis Adams, Jr., Mark Twain, and William Croffut, sixty-three; Thomas Bailey Aldrich, sixty-two; William Dean Howells, sixty-one; William Lloyd Garrison, Jr., sixty; Wendell Phillips Garrison and William Graham Sumner, fifty-eight; William James, fifty-six; Richard Watson Gilder, fifty-four; and Moorfield Storey, fifty-three.*

These mugwump anti-imperialists—men full of years, long experienced as critics and political independents, and unshakably convinced that they were the authentic spokesmen of old-line America—were not inclined to look kindly on imperialism or to shrink from denouncing its sponsors. They were gentlemen of the old school, representatives of a past era, and imperialism did not appeal to them as an exciting new national adventure. In their view the tone of American life had deteriorated lamentably since the Civil War; it pained them to reflect that New England's most famous figures were no longer Daniel Webster, Theodore Parker, and Ralph Waldo Emerson, but "The Beast" Ben Butler, Dwight L. Moody, and P. T. Barnum. They sensed without fully understanding that the growth of industrialism was at the root of the change, and they bemoaned the spectacle of the new and ostentatious rich—flaunting their ill-gotten wealth, corrupting the taste of the nation, and shoving aside the old leaders of public opinion and guardians of public power. Their contempt for the *nouveaux riches* did not ally them

* It might be worthwhile to note here the ages of some of the older non-mugwump anti-imperialists, as of 1898: Justin Morrill, eighty-eight; George S. Boutwell, eighty; Edward Everett Hale, seventy-six; John Sherman, seventy-five; George F. Hoar and John B. Henderson, seventy-two; George F. Edmunds, seventy-one; Benjamin Harrison, sixty-five; Andrew Carnegie, sixty-three; Eugene Hale, sixty-two; Thomas B. Reed, fifty-nine; John Lancaster Spalding, Fifty-eight; and Hermann von Holst, fifty-seven.

with those others who felt more immediately wronged by the wealthy, namely the European immigrant and the workingman. On the contrary, most mugwumps were alarmed by the sight of hordes of poor and untutored Europeans crowding the Anglo-Saxon cities of America. They viewed the laborer with fear because he represented a proletarian side of American civilization which they preferred not to acknowledge and because he was the potential harbinger of social revolution. Even William James, the genial Harvard psychologist and philosopher, and probably as sanguine and tolerant as any mugwump, called the 1886 Haymarket Riot in Chicago "the work of a lot of pathological Germans and Poles." And Charles Eliot Norton, who advocated using state militia to break industrial strikes, called the Pullman Strike of 1894 the most "wrongheaded since the world began" and declared that Eugene Debs, its leader, was a latter-day counterpart of "the mediaeval baron who levied war on the roads." . . .

The mugwumps felt dislike and contempt not only for swarming immigrants and striking railroaders but also for the methods and manners of the businessmen of the age. As early as 1868, E. L. Godkin had commented upon "the immorality which pervades the commercial world, and taints nearly every branch of business." Charles Francis Adams, Jr., who more than any other member of his family entered into America's new commercial life, recorded in his memoirs what must be some of the most scornful lines ever penned about American businessmen:

> As I approach the end, I am more than a little puzzled to account for the instances I have seen of business success—money-getting. It comes from a rather low instinct. Certainly, so far as my observation goes, it is rarely met with in combination with the finer or more interesting traits of character. I have known, and known tolerably well, a good many "successful" men—"big" financially—men famous during the last half-century; and a less interesting crowd I do not care to encounter. Not one that I have ever known would I care to meet again, either in this world or the next; nor is one of them associated in my mind with the idea of humor, thought or refinement. A set of mere money-getters and traders, they were essentially unattractive and uninteresting.

Ever since the Civil War, in the opinion of these mugwumps, humorless, grasping, and uncouth businessmen and the growing industrial masses had been corrupting the taste and tone of the nation. Evidence of the cultural decline was visible on all sides. Charles Eliot Norton bewailed the lack of good literature, the absence of good taste everywhere, while Godkin characterized the men of ill-gotten wealth as a "gaudy stream of bespangled, belaced, and beruffled barbarians" who knew well enough how to enrich themselves ("Plenty of people know how to get money") but who had no "culture," no "imagination," and no "character," and thus were incapable of being "properly" rich.

Of all the social evils in America, corruption and machine control in politics attracted the special attention of the mugwumps. This one problem encompassed a number of others which preoccupied these men—the decline in political morality, the influence of businessmen in politics, and the place of the immigrant in America. E. L. Godkin once characterized politicians as "lewd fellows of the baser sort" and charged in 1884 that James G. Blaine had "wallowed in spoils like a rhinoceros in an African pool." That political life had degenerated to such a point that it appealed almost solely to "lewd fellows" was owing, he thought, to the growth of the political machine, an institution which represented the ultimate triumph of the idea "that one's own party is the best party to have power." The principle of party loyalty stifled all open discussion and debate within the party organization. It paved the way for the machine boss who paid no heed to the needs of society or the wishes of the "intelligent" voter when he personally selected candidates for public office to suit his own nefarious purposes. . . .

By far the most damaging criticism which could be raised against the mugwumps was that, in their preoccupation with such matters as civil morality and public manners, even with tariff reform and "sound money," they neglected to face the truly crucial problems of their day, problems that sorely needed the attention of men of their position and intelligence. Instead of bringing their superior capabilities and considerable influence to bear on the issues that affected the New Americans, the farmers, and the workers, they shrank in disgust from the teeming immigrant population, ridiculed the simple economics of the agrarians, and urged the state militia and federal army to discipline the striking industrial workers. Rather than directly confront the central social and political issues of post–Civil War America, they "seemed constantly to be engaged, heroically enough, in minor skirmishes while the real battles for the control of the government raged elsewhere." It was William Allen White who observed that the mugwumps wanted reform only "in a certain vague, inarticulate, bullfrog fashion." The tame nature of their reform activities was a reflection of their habitual concentration upon the margin rather than the center of American life.

It took the issue of American imperialism in 1898–1900 to arouse the fears of the mugwumps and bring them back to the center of political controversy. They held that the price of expansion abroad would be the repudiation of America's past and the abandonment of her special place in the world—a coin too valuable to pay. In their campaign against imperialism, the mugwumps made their last great fight and returned to the heart of national affairs for the last time. . . .

The anti-imperialists offered a wide range of objections to the acquisition of new territories. They may be summarized as constitutional, economic, diplomatic, moral, racial, political, and historical.

A large number of anti-imperialists believed that imperialism violated the United States Constitution. Some simply contended that the spirit of the Constitution had been contradicted, that it was not right for a government based upon principles of representative rule and the protection of individual liberties to govern other peoples without regard for these principles. Assurances that American colonial rule would be humane did not mollify them, since they believed that benevolence arbitrarily offered could be just as arbitrarily withdrawn. Those who are convinced that imperialism violated not only the spirit but the letter of the Constitution averred that neither Congress nor the President possessed the legal authority to pass laws or set rules for the governing of colonial peoples which were not in strict accord with those established for the people of the United States themselves. Thus Benjamin Harrison, protesting that there could not be one law for the citizen and another for the subject, held that it was unconstitutional for Congress to impose a tariff on goods entering the continental United States from the territory of Puerto Rico; his position was summarized in the popular phrase, "the Constitution follows the flag." The Supreme Court, however, somewhat ambiguously affirmed Congress' extra-constitutional powers in the colonies in the "Insular Cases" of 1901, a verdict that reportedly prompted Elihu Root, the urbane Secretary of War, to comment: "Ye-es, as near as I can make out the Constitution follows the flag—but doesn't quite catch up with it."

In making an economic case against imperialism, critics denied the truth of another contemporary aphorism, to wit, that "trade follows the flag." Men like Carl Schurz and Andrew Carnegie felt that it was unnecessary to plant the flag in the spongy soil of the tropics in order to capture the area's trade. The laws of commerce would determine how successful the Americans were in selling their surplus abroad. If they found profitable markets it would be because the products of their mills, mines, factories, and farms were cheap and attractive enough to compete with those of other nations and not because they had seized and roped off markets for their exclusive use. Occasionally an anti-imperialist would add that a reduced tariff schedule which allowed foreigners a better opportunity to sell their wares in the United States would enhance their ability to purchase American goods in return and thus promote a greater increase in American exports than McKinley's policy of imperialism.

Businessmen Andrew Carnegie and Edward Atkinson suggested additional economic reasons for rejecting an annexationist policy. According to the former, any effort to regularize commercial relations within an American empire would be accompanied by hopeless economic and political difficulties. Free trade between the United States and the Philippines would bankrupt American farmers and certain groups of raw material producers, yet a tariff on the colony's goods would violate the Constitution and destroy the islands' economy. To open the market of the Philippines on equal terms to the United States and other nations would fulfill the principle of the open door but would ruin American exporters who had to pay heavier transportation charges than those incurred by their German, British, and Australian competitors. If, on the other hand, the Philippines market were kept exclusively for the United States the resulting anger of European powers interested in Far Eastern trade would produce a dangerous diplomatic crisis.

Edward Atkinson took another tack. For years he had been an eager advocate of increased economic activity in Latin America and the Far East, but in 1899 he concluded that the prize of Oriental trade (and, to a certain extent, of Latin American trade) was not worth the cost of acquiring it. There would be time enough to bid for those markets when China and other undeveloped nations had industrialized and generated enough purchasing power to buy in quantity the kind of sophisticated goods that the United States produced. In the meantime more significant profits could be made from trade with America's traditional partners, the industrial nations of Europe and Canada.

Anti-imperialists also objected to a policy of colonialism because it threatened to involve America more deeply in international politics, especially in Asia. They abhorred this prospect on three counts. First, it was a contradiction of their conception of American diplomatic traditions, a departure from the path of non-entanglement laid down by the founders of the nation and a negation of the Monroe Doctrine, which they interpreted as meaning "Europe for the Europeans" and "Asia for the Asians" as well as "America for the Americans." Secondly, involvement in Asian imperial politics would endanger the security of the United States. Anti-imperialists charged that by extending American responsibility to Hawaii and the Philippines, the McKinley administration had broken the nation's ocean belt of security and placed the flag in outlying regions where it was vulnerable to intimidation or attack by other powers. With its security no longer ensured by geography, the United States would have to build an enormous navy and an army of respectable strength to protect its new possessions against any action that seemed to threaten them, however remotely. Thirdly, the domestic repercussions of a leading role in world politics would prove costly. Future wars and the permanent maintenance of forces strong enough to wage them would require a vast amount of money, discourage industry, impose heavy tax burdens on the American people, and distract attention from the solution of domestic problems that had a far greater bearing on the future than any foreign policy issues could have—problems of race and radicalism, currency and the cities, trusts and the tariff.

The moral critique of the anti-imperialists requires few words to summarize although it was just as important as their constitutional, economic, or strategic objections to imperialism. They believed—simply, genuinely, and emphatically— that it was *wrong* for the United States forcibly to impose its will on other peoples. No economic or diplomatic reasoning could justify slaughtering Filipinos who wanted their independence. No standard of justice or morality would sustain the transformation of a war that had begun as a crusade to liberate Cuba from Spanish tyranny into a campaign of imperialist conquest.

As genuine if not as high-minded were the racial attitudes that contributed to the anti-imperialist stand. With a few rare exceptions like George Hoar, the opponents of imperialism shared entirely the expansionists' belief in the inferiority and incapacity of the world's colored races (and of some that were not colored). But while those in the imperialist camp usually proceeded from these racist assumptions to a belief in the duty of Americans to uplift and care for the backward and benighted savages of Puerto Rico and the Philippines, the anti-imperialists appealed to these same assumptions to justify excluding such peoples from a place in the American political system. They believed that the United States should belong to its own kind, the Anglo-Saxons (or "Germanic" races as Carl Schurz would have it). The blood of tropical peoples would taint the stream of American political and social life and further complicate the nation's already festering racial problems. As the *New York World* asked on June 19, 1898, did the United States, which already had a "black elephant" in the South, "really need a white elephant in the Philippines, a leper elephant in Hawaii, a brown elephant in Porto Rico and perhaps a yellow elephant in Cuba?"

In their political objections to expansionism the anti-imperialists were guided by abstract principles. For the most part they were political fundamentalists—they believed in the literal truth and universal applicability of the ideas of liberty and republican government. Free of the skepticism and self-consciousness of later generations, they asserted that a republican government could not also be an imperial government; that the rule of self-government did not permit exceptions in faraway territories; that freedom was a value of universal appeal, in the Philippines and Puerto Rico as well as in the United States; and that all men, whatever their attainments and wherever they lived, possessed the right to enjoy the blessings of freedom. The United States could not preserve its own democracy if it denied the right of self-rule to others.

Finally, anti-imperialists had what might be called historical motives for opposing imperialism. Most of them were traditionalists who believed imperialism to be in sharp conflict with established ideals and practices. Acquiring overseas colonies and joining the worldwide struggle for power and empire were inconsistent with American diplomatic traditions, with America's historic identification with the ideal of liberty, and with the lofty notion that America should serve the world not through force but through the force of her example. Imperialism destroyed the unquestioned belief in American innocence and uniqueness.

The anti-imperialists were primarily and overwhelmingly concerned with their own country—its security, prosperity, constitutional integrity, and moral and political health—and not with the fate of Filipinos, Cubans, Hawaiians, or Puerto Ricans. Although they could and did defend the rights of these peoples, their fundamental purpose was to defend the interests of the United States. . . .

The failure of the anti-imperialists to prevent the expansionists' victory of 1898–1900 had several causes. The most obvious was simply their inability to persuade their countrymen of the truth of their dire forecasts.

Hitches, flaws, inconsistencies, and compromises in their own activities and arguments weakened the anti-imperialist position. Those who listened to Carl Schurz must have been confused by the fact that he alternated between an insistence upon immediate and full independence for the new possessions and schemes for setting up protectorates until the inhabitants were "ready" for independence. No matter how honest his motives or practical his objectives, Charles Francis Adams' attack on his fellow anti-imperialists in the spring of 1899 certainly did the movement no good in the eyes of the general public. Nor did the strained logic revealed by Andrew Carnegie and many others when they declared imperialism wrong as a matter of principle but stood firm only against the annexation of the Philippines. Or George Hoar's willingness to accept an expansionist victory by default in Hawaii prior to putting up a real fight against the annexation of the Philippines and Puerto Rico. How impressive could the anti-imperialists be when Benjamin Harrison waited until the dust had settled from the 1900 campaign before entraining for Ann Arbor to make his tardy declaration against imperialism? Or when "Czar"

Reed, at the very moment when his voice and influence were badly needed by other anti-imperialists, quit Congress for moneymaking and the scribbling of ironical anti-imperialist memos that never left the privacy of his study?

President McKinley's own actions made it difficult for the anti-imperialists to translate their moral and idealistic fervor into a political force strong enough to block his program. Understanding a President's tremendous power to take the political initiative, McKinley committed the United States to a series of *faits accomplis* before any effective protest could be made: ordering Dewey to Manila Bay, sending American troops to the Philippines to secure the results of the Commodore's triumph, and dispatching a compliant peace commission to Paris to negotiate the treaty. These events occurred within the space of a few months, and it would have taken an extraordinarily strong, united, and determined lot of anti-imperialists to check the President during this period.

But anti-imperialists were in no such position of strength and unity. The Democrats were at a disadvantage because they had bellowed for war in 1898 as loudly as anyone, because Bryan had intervened in behalf of the peace treaty, and because their party had no other leader of national importance who could take charge of a bi-partisan anti-imperialist coalition aimed at defeating the treaty. The impact of the mugwumps was limited by their disunity on objectives and their position as independent critics standing completely aloof from the national party system. Suspicious of the wiles of professional politicians and hostile to compromise, they spent valuable time reciting the past errors of both Republicans and Democrats, thus courting trouble in broadening the base of their support. The Republican anti-imperialists, on the other hand, were hamstrung by partisanship. It prevented either Hoar or Harrison from making full-fledged commitments to the movement. Hoar, who refused to consider taking the lead of any but a pure Republican protest, spent an inordinate amount of time fending off and quarreling with mugwumps and justifying McKinley to other anti-imperialists. Harrison, though full of venom against the President, delayed attacking his administration until December, 1900, precisely because he wished to do nothing that would cause it political damage.

Another handicap facing the anti-imperialists in their attempts to influence public opinion was the matter of age—their average age was over sixty-nine years. Men born in the 1820s and 1830s were unlikely to have great powers of persuasion over a nation just entering a brave new century.

Finally, the anti-imperialists labored under the disadvantage of having the negative side of the debate. They had to say no, to ask a people aroused by American armed triumphs to surrender the fruits of victory. They had "to blow cold upon the hot excitement," as William James put it. Failure came in part because it was not possible to make Americans ashamed of themselves and afraid of the future at a time when they were enjoying fresh breezes of prosperity, glory, and optimism after more than a decade of depression and social strife. The anti-imperialists had run headlong into the fact that nothing succeeds like success. . . .

The historian has the duty to judge as well as analyze and describe. Besides appraising their impact on America it is necessary to appraise the anti-imperialists themselves and weigh both their errors and their achievements.

As political tacticians they are vulnerable to criticism, not only because they failed to maintain a united front (the result of honest disagreements) but also because they took a perverse delight in airing their differences in public. This open squabbling spoke well for their irrepressible individualism and their faith in free debate but not so well for their political judgment. They made another tactical error by reacting to all their opponents as if they were headstrong and romantic belligerents like Theodore Roosevelt and Albert Beveridge. The more cautious and influential, like McKinley and Hay, saw no way to escape from the Philippines, and perhaps did not even want to, but they had no interest in studying the map for new lands to conquer. In fact, when McKinley sent civilian commissions to the Philippines to study the problems of governing the islands, he twice appointed as chairmen men who had originally opposed annexing them, Jacob G. Schurman and William Howard Taft. Anti-imperialists certainly had grounds for disagreement with the administration, but few of them understood how narrow the grounds of opposition were on certain issues.

The anti-imperialists may be criticized as diplomatic strategists and as advocates of alternative policies that were notably impracticable. It is the virtually unanimous judgment of diplomatic historians that there was no politic way to get out of the Philippines after Dewey's naval victory of May 1, 1898. The American people would have rejected returning the islands to Spain as a perfidious betrayal of those Filipinos who had cooperated in the American victory at Manila. A protectorate, a favorite scheme of some of the more prominent anti-imperialists, would have committed the United States to involvement in the Far East without providing it with the power necessary to exercise its responsibilities. Ceding the Philippines to a foreign power other than Spain would have sparked fierce resentment among other nations and endangered the peace of the area. It is highly unlikely that it would have been possible to create any kind of international consortium to guarantee the neutrality and protect the security of the Philippines, or to make it work if it could have been created. Giving the Philippines immediate independence and then leaving them to their own devices might have touched off a general Asian war among the great powers with interests in the Far East, a war into which the United States would almost surely have been drawn. One can only speculate on these matters, of course, but there is little assurance that Aguinaldo and his followers could have united the Filipinos behind them and established a workable system of self-government and even less that they could have resisted falling prey to the aggression of another country. As George F. Kennan has written:

The alternative to the establishment of American power in the Philippines . . . was not a nice, free, progressive Philippine Republic: it was Spanish, German, or Japanese domination. Abstention on our part from the taking of the Philippines could have been argued, and was, from the standpoint of our interests; it could scarcely have been argued from the interests of the Filipinos themselves.

As prophets the anti-imperialists also fell into error. Three of their most important prophecies were proved wrong by the passage of time. Undemocratic modes of colonial rule did not produce a tyrannical backlash in the United States. The annexation of the Philippines, Hawaii, and Puerto Rico, although foreshadowing a long-term extension of American interests in Asia and three decades of interventionist diplomacy in Central America and the Caribbean, did not lead to a continuing orgy of territorial expansion. And American colonial rule, however imperfect, was not characterized by incompetence, corruption, brutality, or injustice. Perhaps because the United States had no vital need to exploit the resources of its colonies it made a record as imperial master which, compared with traditional European examples, was notably intelligent, restrained, and humane.

There is also the question of whether the anti-imperialists failed as moralists. Christopher Lasch, noting that many anti-imperialists believed the Filipinos unfit for self-government by American standards, charges that they were "un-Christian" in wanting to abandon the natives to their own fate. This criticism fails to reckon with what most anti-imperialists thought the consequences of independence would be. Despite their prevailing assumption that Filipinos were not as competent in political matters as their American masters, the anti-imperialists did not believe that independence would be followed by anarchy, misery, and resumed foreign domination. Impressed by Aguinaldo's talent in setting up his own insurrectionary "republic" and leading the fight against American forces, the advocates of independence were convinced that their policy would lead, not to disaster, but to the founding of an independent Philippine republic. Had the Filipinos tried and failed in their attempt to govern themselves and fend off foreign pressures, the anti-imperialists would have been proved wrong as prophets, not as moralists.

They can be condemned as racists. Whether they used words like "superior" and "inferior" or "civilized" and "uncivilized," they thought of peoples in the categories of racism. George Hoar was generally an exception, but even he gave himself over to this kind of thinking on occasion. The unhappy fact is that few Americans were immune to the prevailing racism of the late nineteenth century. The anti-imperialists were no better or worse than their countrymen.

The anti-imperialists also left much to be desired in their role as guardians of and spokesmen for the nation's ideals. Their idealism and selflessness were too often offset by a narrow conservatism and meanness of spirit. Their motives were both noble and ignoble, their declarations both grand and picayune. At times they seemed to be men with little faith in the resiliency of their own nation. Although they claimed to regard it as the most wonderful on earth, they made it sound like one of the most fragile. How much faith could Carl Schurz have had in the strength and viability of America's vaunted democratic principles and institutions if he believed that colonial rule in the Philippines would rapidly erode the principles or that Puerto Rican statehood would inexorably poison the institutions?

Finally, the anti-imperialists failed to offer an alternative vision of the nation's future. Criticizing the new expansionist conception of America's place in international affairs, they prescribed nothing more enticing than a return to the past. They knew that the annexation of faraway territories and alien peoples

was inconsistent with America's past traditions, but it did not occur to them
to question the continued worth and relevance of the traditions themselves.
Making no effort to remold the American heritage in new patterns and adapt
it to the twentieth century, they served notice that an imperial career would
signal the end of the America that had been. They did not offer a vision of
what America could become.

There is also much to praise in the anti-imperialist record. Later events
vindicated their prediction that the possession of Pacific colonies would weaken
rather than strengthen the diplomatic and military position of the United
States. As early as 1907 President Theodore Roosevelt acknowledged that the
distant and poorly defended Philippines were the "heel of Achilles" of
American policy in the Far East and considered announcing to the world
that they would soon be given their independence. Nothing of the sort was
done, however, and for forty years the islands remained a hostage to American
strategy in Asia, complicating and inhibiting policy *vis-à-vis* Japan from the
time of Theodore Roosevelt to Franklin Roosevelt. When Japanese-American
relations finally degenerated into open hostility, war commenced with a
Japanese strike at the two exposed flanks of American power—Hawaii and
the Philippines, the gains of 1898.

A judgment on the anti-imperialists' contention that colonies would not
add important strength to the American economy depends upon one's
definition of the word "important." Individual firms and industries obviously
profited from the colonies while many others were quite unaffected by the
new order. What is clear, however, is that Edward Atkinson and others were
correct in their belief that imperial possessions would not measurably enhance
the health and vigor of the American economy. Exports to Latin America
and the Far East have increased significantly in the course of the twentieth
century, as have capital investments, but the increase has been a general one,
not restricted to or explainable by America's presence in her new colonies.

Although the anti-imperialists were wrong in their dark predictions of what
would happen in the United States as a direct result of colonialism abroad, their
political logic on this point was irrefutable. There *is* no answer to their charge
that a nation that believes in representative government has no business ruling
other peoples against their consent, no matter how gentle the rule or how
little it impinges on the lives of the people in the mother country. "Kings
can have subjects; it is a question whether a republic can," George Kennan
has remarked, adding:

*If it is true that our society is really capable of knowing only the
quantity which we call "citizen," that it debauches its own innermost
nature when it tries to deal with the quantity called "subject," then the
potential scope of our system is limited; then it can extend only to people
of our own kind—people who have grown up in the same peculiar
spirit of independence and self-reliance, people who can accept, and
enjoy, and content themselves with our institutions. In this case, the
ruling of distant peoples is not our dish.*

One could have hoped that men as intelligent, as broad in their vision, as socially established as the leading anti-imperialists might have succeeded in transcending the racist thinking of their times. Yet even their racism was more realistic than the patronizing policies of uplift offered by the expansionists because it took into account the difficulty Americans would have in dealing with "inferior" races. Charles Francis Adams was scornful of prattle about the "white man's burden" and "lifting up inferior races." Considering the "unchristian, brutal, exterminating" treatment the Indian had been subjected to by American settlers and the nation's "long, shameful record" with Negroes and Chinese, it was ridiculous to think of the United States as in any way specially fitted to govern less familiar peoples. Adams was right. The bloody streak of racial tension evident throughout the history of the United States, the all-too-evident fact that the streak is nowhere near its end, the inability of Americans abroad (soldiers and civilians) to resist stereotyping colored peoples as "little brown brothers," "chinks," "Japs," "gooks," or whatever—all this points to the conclusion that the "Anglo-Saxon" majority of the United States has found it unusually difficult to deal with people of other races and cultures. America's relatively good record as colonial ruler was not the result of an abandonment of racism but the product of ideals and circumstances that operated in spite of racist thinking. Racism, in fact, caused some of the worst blots on that colonial record.

There was a great need in 1899 and 1900 for someone to challenge the self-congratulatory paternalism of expansionists in the Philippines, who explained that the bloody spanking they were administering to the childish but devious natives was for the latters' own good. The anti-imperialists provided the moral challenge to this arrogant and expedient explanation. William James, remarking the ease with which imperialists justified killing in the name of political abstractions, launched devastating attacks against the amorality and pointlessness of Theodore Roosevelt's love of violence and struggle. Even earlier Charles Eliot Norton had warned that the United States could not escape guilt by punishing Spanish murder in Cuba with still more death. The moral dilemmas and ironies of imperialism were perhaps never dissected more expertly than by Finley Peter Dunne's "Mr. Dooley," who declaimed:

We say to thim: "Naygurs," we say, "poor, dissolute, uncovered wretches," says we, "whin th' crool hand iv Spain forged man'cles f'r ye'er limbs, as Hogan says, who was it crossed th' say an' sthruck off th' comealongs? We did,—by dad, we did. An' now, ye mis'rable, childish-minded apes, we propose f'r to larn ye th' uses iv liberty. In ivry city in this unfair land we will erect schoolhouses an' packin' houses an' houses iv correction; an' we'll larn ye our language, because 'tis aisier to larn ye ours than to larn oursilves yours. An' we'll give ye clothes, if ye pay f'r thim; an', if ye don't, ye can go without."

The anti-imperialists displayed admirable spirit in making their protest in the face of hostile public opinion. They constantly encountered bitter criticism, including the accusation that they were encouraging the Filipino rebels in their resistance to American authority and thus indirectly causing the deaths of American soldiers. The *New York Times* declared: "The Anti-Imperialist

League might go one step further. It might send rifles, Maxim guns, and stores of
ammunition to the Filipinos . . . it would be more openly and frankly
treasonable." The commander of the New York chapter of the Grand Army of
the Republic proclaimed in 1899 that anti-imperialists were unworthy of "the
protection of the flag they dishonor and . . . the name of American citizens."
After his June 7, 1898, address on "True Patriotism," Charles Eliot Norton
was the target of abusive letters and public scoldings, even from George Hoar,
a fellow anti-imperialist. One correspondent informed him that "there are
stray bullets somewhere that are liable to hit our country's enemies," and
another simply warned: "You had better pull out[.] Yours with contempt—
A white man." The *Chicago Tribune,* not passing up a chance to criticize an
eastern professor, accused Norton of trying "to kill the generous impulses of
patriotism and to besmirch the noble cause of humanity upon which the war
against Spain is based." Vice-President Roosevelt in 1901 described the
anti-imperialists in a letter as "simply unhung traitors, and . . . liars, slanderers
and scandalmongers to boot." Dissent in the face of such condemnation was an
act of considerable moral courage.

Above all the anti-imperialists served their countrymen well by reminding
them of their own identity and purpose in the world. Knowing that it was a
departure from traditional American practice to acquire distant, heavily
populated colonies for which statehood was not intended, they also understood
the deeper significance of this change—that it denoted America's intention to
take a place among the great powers of the world in active international politics.
The anti-imperialists deserve credit for drawing attention to the magnitude of
this new departure, for pointing out the political and moral problems that
would follow in its wake, and for refusing to concede that America's new
status must necessarily mean the abandonment of her traditional practices.
Great powers are not expected to conduct themselves like YMCA counselors.
This the anti-imperialists did not fully appreciate, but they did hold out the
hope that great power could yield, not greed and amorality, but a sense of
national security and a record of justice and magnanimity.

The anti-imperialists' concern was always more with the morality and justice
of American policy than with the diplomatic decisions and judgments that
influenced it. It was partly for this reason that they were unable to propose
feasible alternative policies. But this is not a fatal shortcoming in movements
of this sort. Their primary accomplishment was to lodge a protest, to demand
answers to moral questions that were hard and perhaps impossible to answer,
to reassert traditional American ideals. The anti-imperialists are still a
reminder of the value of conservative dissent; with their concern for America's
traditional values and their own ideological heritage, they were better able
than the less historically minded to compare present performance with past
principle and then ask: Do they match? Can they be reconciled?

Their answers did not always satisfy a people nurtured on optimism and
faith in progress. Their conservatism often prevented them from appreciating the
beneficial effects change could have on their nation. Even so, they did comprehend
the need for a changing society to remain aware of its founding principles.
They understood that a nation that violated its own declared purposes could be

wrenched from its moral and spiritual moorings. The anti-imperialists knew that a democratic people were ill-suited to a career as colonialists. They knew that war and imperialism could have unfortunate and unpredictable effects on their own nation and that a preoccupation with problems halfway around the world might divert important national resources to unworthy ends, lower standards of government and political conduct, cause the neglect of pressing domestic problems, and even alter the moral foundations of society itself.

When Charles Francis Adams expressed his misgivings during the Spanish-American War, he was told, "Oh, no!—such ideas are 'pessimistic'; you should have more faith in the American people!" These reassurances came from a people who believed they were beyond the reach of history—that they could live forever and that nothing could ever happen to their liberties and privileges. The anti-imperialists found it difficult to see far into the future, but at least they knew that it could bring decay, deterioration, and the perversion of principle just as easily as endless progress. It was their office, their purpose, and their achievement to warn a nation of optimists that America could not escape the consequences of its own conduct.

eleven
the anti-imperialist
as racist

CHRISTOPHER LASCH

*Most historians agree that racism and bigotry were vigorous
in the United States of the late nineteenth century; few
of America's 9 million Negroes could identify with the
1900 Republican party platform's enthusiastic endorsement
of the results of the war: "To ten millions of the
human race there was given 'a new birth of freedom' and
to the American people a new and noble responsibility."
Christopher Lasch (b. 1932), professor of history at
the University of Rochester, notes in this article that the
anti-imperialists, like the imperialists, were ardent partakers
of the prevalent racism. He stresses similarities rather
than differences between the two groups. Lasch has written
on a wide range of topics, but has emphasized American
dissenters in his research. Among his publications are*
American Liberals and the Russian Revolution *(1962)*,
The New Radicalism in America *(1965)*, and The Agony
of the American Left *(1969)*.

The cession of the Philippine Islands to the United States
precipitated a great debate on the nature of our foreign
policy and our national destiny. Opinion on the wisdom of
retaining the Philippines was divided without regard to
party or section; indeed, the intrusion of the expansionist
issue into the politics of the period tended for a time to
obliterate sectionalism. Yet sectional considerations,
particularly in the South, were not absent from the debate.
Southern Democrats were almost unanimous in condemning
"imperialism," on the grounds that Asiatics, like Negroes,

Source: Christopher Lasch, "The Anti-Imperialists, the Philippines,
and the Inequality of Man," *Journal of Southern History* 24
(August 1958): 319–31. Used by permission of the *Journal of
Southern History.*

were innately inferior to white people and could not be assimilated to American life. Two decades earlier such arguments would have called forth angry rejoinders from the North. That the South's recourse to them at the end of the century did not revive the old controversy over Reconstruction revealed the extent to which Northern liberals had retreated from the implications of their emancipation of the Negro—a retreat the irony of which Southern statesmen never tired of expounding. An examination of the debate over imperialism helps to explain this remarkable change in Northern opinion and thereby enables us to see Southern racialism, so prevalent in the nineties, in a larger perspective. Thus a revaluation of an experience essentially national, not sectional, compels a revaluation of sectional history as well. Just as the corruption of the Reconstruction governments was paralleled by corruption in Northern state governments and in Washington, as historians are beginning to show, so at a somewhat later date illiberalism in the South also had its counterpart in the North. The retreat from idealism was a national, not a local, phenomenon.

That Northerners of the expansionist persuasion made no reply to those who in the course of challenging the annexation of the Philippines challenged some of the fundamental assumptions of American democracy should come as no surprise. The expansionists were in a delicate predicament. Men who favored acquiring the Philippines on the grounds that the natives were unfit for self-government could hardly afford to apply another logic to the Negro problem in the South; Senator Henry Cabot Lodge, among others, might well look back on his recent Force Bill as a youthful indiscretion which it were prudent to forget. But one would not have expected anti-imperialists in the North to share this reluctance to revive the dispute over equality. Because they professed a fervid devotion to the rights of man, the anti-imperialists might have been expected to guide the debate over annexation to higher ground by rejecting outright the leading argument both of the expansionists and of the Southern antiexpansionists, namely that men are created unequal. Most historians have in fact assumed that anti-imperialism was genuinely liberal in inspiration and that the anti-imperialists were voicing objections to colonialism now commonly accepted.

The position of the anti-imperialists does at first appear to have been sensible and straightforward: that is, that imperialism was not only inexpedient but unjust, a departure from the historic principles of the Declaration of Independence. But a closer examination of certain facets of anti-imperialism may require us to see the anti-imperialists in a rather different light. Their argument did not foreshadow the liberalism of the Good Neighbor policy. It was in fact no more liberal than that of the expansionists. Indeed, it resembled the expansionist rationale, against which it appeared to be a protest, far more closely than it does any of the objections we might today raise against a colonial policy, or for that matter than it resembled the theories of Thomas Jefferson. It was a product of the late nineteenth century, not of the eighteenth or twentieth centuries. The anti-imperialists, like the imperialists, saw the world from a pseudo-Darwinian point of view. They accepted the inequality of man—or, to be more precise, of races—as an established fact of life. They did not question the idea that Anglo-Saxons were superior to other people, and some of them would even have agreed that they were destined eventually to conquer the world. They did not quarrel with the idea of "destiny"; they merely refused to believe that destiny required such strenuous exertions of the American people, particularly when they saw in those exertions the menace of militarism and tyranny. There were important differences of opinion, of course, between those who favored and those who opposed the annexation of the Philippines, but for the moment it is perhaps more important to dwell on the matters on which they agreed. Most middle-class Americans of the 1890's agreed in attaching great importance to the concept of race, and it was that agreement which gave the intellectual life of the period its peculiar tone.

It is characteristic of the period that neither side in the debate over the Philippines was content to rest its case on considerations of expediency alone, although the expansionist clique on whom defense of the "large policy" devolved tried to rouse the business community, which was apathetic toward the whole question of expansion, with visions of glittering markets in China. But economic arguments could too easily be attacked as sordid, and the expansionists preferred to stand on higher ground. They appealed to "manifest destiny," an old idea, and to the newer, post-Darwinian idea that it was the manifest *duty* of higher civilizations to displace lower ones, either through outright elimination (as the white man had eliminated the Indian) or through a process of uplift and "Christianization." It was as carriers of civilization, they argued, that the American people were obliged to annex the Philippines, however disagreeable the obligation might appear.

The anti-imperialists, largely ignoring the economic and strategic arguments for annexation, replied with a moral argument of their own. They admitted that our history, as the expansionists were fond of showing, was a record of territorial expansion, but they fixed the limits of our westward destiny at the shores of the Pacific. The American destiny, they contended, was merely continental, not global. All of the areas previously acquired by the United States had been on the North American continent, and all except Alaska had been contiguous to the old states. Because they were contiguous and because they were thinly populated, they came to be settled by citizens from the older states, by white, Protestant, English-speaking people—by a population, in short, indistinguishable from that of the older states. The new territories, therefore, could be, and were, admitted to statehood. (Alaska, again, was the single exception.)

But to annex distant islands already heavily populated by racial aliens, the anti-imperialists maintained, would be a momentous and disastrous departure from the past. The Filipinos, for any number of reasons, could not become American citizens; they would have to be governed as subjects. But how could a republic have subjects? For the United States to acquire the Philippines without admitting their people to full citizenship would amount to government without the consent of the governed—a flat contradiction of the cardinal principle of American democracy, the principle over which we separated from England, the principle of the Declaration of Independence. Nor was this all. As a result of the initial injustice, others would follow. A large standing army would have to be created in order to defend our new possessions not only against foreign powers but against the natives themselves, who were already in revolt against American rule; and an army called into being for the purpose of crushing freedom abroad would ultimately be used to destroy it at home. The administration had already begun to censor news from the Philippines, in order to create the impression that the hostilities there were purely defensive in character, and the anti-imperialists saw in this an evil omen—proof that if the United States persisted in imperialism, she would eventually go the way of Rome.

The exponents of annexation could offer no satisfactory answer to all this. Instead, they attempted to create a dilemma of their own—to show that there was no satisfactory alternative to annexation. Accordingly they argued that the Filipinos were not "ready" for self-government and if left to themselves would fall into the hands of a native dictator or a foreign conqueror. But not a single expansionist proposed that the privileges of citizenship be extended to the Philippines. They assumed that the Filipinos would have to be governed as second-class citizens, and with that assumption they departed from the natural-rights philosophy of the Declaration of Independence, exactly as their antagonists accused them of doing. Senator Henry M. Teller, an expansionist, confessed that to hold the islanders as subjects would be "rather objectionable in a republic"; but there seemed no choice. Not all the expansionists had similar reservations, but almost all of them recognized and admitted the implications of their policy for the doctrine of natural rights. In effect, they substituted for the Jeffersonian proposition that the right to liberty is "natural"—hence universal— the proposition that rights depend on environment—on "civilization," of which there were now seen to be many stages of development; on race; even on climate. A pseudo-Darwinian hierarchy of cultural stages, unequal in the capacity for enjoyment of the rights associated with self-government, replaced the simpler and more liberal theory of the Enlightenment, which recognized only the distinction between society and nature. "Rights," as absolutes, lost their meaning by becoming relative to time and place. Rights now depended on a people's "readiness" to enjoy them.

It is not surprising that the anti-imperialists accused the expansionists of abandoning the Declaration of Independence. What is surprising is that their own arguments were no closer to the spirit of that document than the ones they denounced with such fervor. The anti-imperialists were in fact no more Jeffersonian in their essential outlook than Theodore Roosevelt or Henry Cabot Lodge or Alfred T. Mahan was, for they did not challenge the central assumption of imperialist thought: the natural inequality of men. The imperialists at least had the merit of consistency; they made no professions of Jeffersonianism. The anti-imperialists, on the other hand, invoked the name of Jefferson at every opportunity.

Some light on the anti-imperialists is shed by the high proportion of Southerners among them. In the Senate, only four of twenty-eight Southern senators favored unconditional ratification of the treaty with Spain, and Southerners led the attack on the treaty in debate. Their arguments against ratification clearly reflected the lingering bitterness of Reconstruction, as well as more recent movements to exclude Negroes from the benefits of citizenship. Annexation of the Philippines, they argued, would merely compound the race problem by introducing into the country what Senator John W. Daniel of Virginia called a "mess of Asiatic pottage." Benjamin R. Tillman of South Carolina was especially active in the anti-imperialist cause, playing ingenious variations on the racial theme. At times he gave it a distinctly Darwinian note: ". . . we [he said, referring to the South] understand and realize what it is to have two races side by side that can not mix or mingle without deterioration and injury to both and the ultimate destruction of the civilization of the higher." At other times he gave it a pro-labor bias: ". . . here are 10,000,000 Asiatics who will have the right as soon as the pending treaty is ratified, to get on the first ship that they can reach and come here and compete in the labor market of the United States." In a more somber mood, he appeared to speak more in sorrow than in anger: ". . . coming . . . as a Senator from . . . South Carolina, with 750,000 colored population and only 500,000 whites, I realize what you are doing, while you don't; and I would save this country from the injection into it of another race question which can only breed bloodshed and a costly war and the loss of the lives of our brave soldiers." More often, however, he spoke with biting irony which revealed the Negro, not the Filipino, as the real source of his anxiety and, further, which showed that he was more interested in embarrassing the North— in forcing its senators to admit to a contradiction—than he was in preventing the acquisition of the Philippines. When Knute Nelson of Minnesota, once an abolitionist, declared that the Filipinos were incapable of self-government, Tillman replied: "I want to call the Senator's attention to the fact, however, that he and others who are now contending for a different policy in Hawaii and the Philippines gave the slaves of the South not only self-government, but they forced on the white men of the South, at the point of the bayonet, the rule and domination of those ex-slaves. Why the difference? Why the change? Do you acknowledge that you were wrong in 1868?"

It is unnecessary to insist that such arguments did not spring from a deep-seated attachment to the Declaration of Independence. But it would be manifestly unfair to judge the whole anti-imperialist movement on the basis of its Southern wing, particularly when many Northern men of the persuasion were clearly uncomfortable at finding themselves in the company of men like Tillman. An examination of their own arguments, however, discloses no important difference from that of the Southerners, except that Northern anti-imperialists did not dwell on the parallel with the Southern Negro problem—something they were by this time anxious to forget. One is left with the impression that it was not the Southern argument as such that disconcerted the Northerners, but the use to which the South put it. When it came to giving reasons why the Philippines should not be annexed, North and South found themselves in close agreement.*

Anti-imperialists contended that the Filipinos, unless they were given their independence, would have to be held in subjection, since they could not be admitted as citizens. What is interesting is the manner in which they arrived at the latter conclusion. A brief study of the process reveals a Darwinism as thoroughgoing as that of the imperialists themselves.

In the first place, the anti-imperialists argued, if the Filipinos became citizens,

---

* A few Northern anti-imperialists, like Moorfield Storey, defended the rights of the Negro, and accordingly did not object to imperialism on racial grounds; but these were rare exceptions.

they would migrate to the United States and compete with American labor—a prospect especially alarming in view of the racial composition of the islands. As Samuel Gompers declared: "If the Philippines are annexed, what is to prevent the Chinese, the Negritos, and the Malays coming to our own country?" This was more than an economic argument. It implied that those people were accustomed to a low standard of living and, what is more, that they were incapable, by virtue of their race, of longing for anything better. It implied that Orientals, in short, would work for low wages because they could not, and never would, appreciate the finer things of life which money alone could buy. This view had already come into vogue on the West Coast, where it was particularly popular with organized labor; it is not surprising, therefore, to find Gompers appealing to it.

If cheap Filipino labor would compete unfairly with American labor, cheap Filipino goods could be expected to compete unfairly with American goods. If we took over the islands, we could neither prevent immigration nor levy protective import duties. Annexation would therefore injure both capital and labor.

But the Filipinos would also be given the vote. Considering, again, the racial composition of the islands, the results would clearly be ruinous. Carl Schurz declared:

If they become states on an equal footing with the other states they will not only be permitted to govern themselves as to their home concerns, but will take part in governing the whole republic, in governing us, by sending senators and representatives into our Congress to help make our laws, and by voting for president and vice-president to give our national government its executive. The prospect of the consequences which would follow the admission of the Spanish creoles and the negroes of the West India islands and of the Malays and Tagals of the Philippines to participation in the conduct of our government is so alarming that you instinctively pause before taking the step.

The same sentiments were expressed by James L. Blair of St. Louis, the son of the old Free Soil leader Francis Preston Blair. "History," Blair said, "shows no instance of a tropical people who have demonstrated a capacity for maintaining an enduring form of Republican government." To admit such a people into a share in the government of the United States would be self-destructive. David Starr Jordan warned his countrymen: "If we govern the Philippines, so in their degree must the Philippines govern us." Or as Champ Clark put it even more forcefully in the House of Representatives: "No matter whether they are fit to govern themselves or not, they are not fit to govern us [applause]."

But if it was undesirable for the Filipinos to come to the United States or to take part in American government, was it not still possible that Americans would emigrate to the Philippines and gradually displace the native culture? The anti-imperialists denied that any such outcome was possible. In the first place, "the two races could never amalgamate"; "the racial differences between the Oriental and Western races are never to be eradicated." But suppose the

Filipinos were eliminated by force or herded into reservations, like the
American Indians. Even then, the anti-imperialists insisted, annexation would be
unwise, for the fact was that neither the "northern" (or "Anglo-Saxon" or
"Germanic") race nor democratic institutions could survive in a tropical
climate. "Civilization," said Jordan, "is, as it were, suffocated in the tropics." On
another occasion he explained that the Philippines "lie in the heart of the torrid
zone, 'Nature's asylum for degenerates.' " "Neither the people nor the institutions
of the United States can ever occupy the Philippines," he said. "The American
home cannot endure there, the town-meeting cannot exist." Schurz echoed the
same refrain:

> *They are . . . situated in the tropics, where people of the northern races,*
> *such as Anglo-Saxons, or generally speaking, people of Germanic blood,*
> *have never migrated in mass to stay; and they are more or less densely*
> *populated, parts of them as densely as Massachusetts—their population*
> *consisting almost exclusively of races to whom the tropical climate is*
> *congenial— . . . Malays, Tagals, Filipinos, Chinese, Japanese, Negritos,*
> *and various more or less barbarous tribes. . . .*

Such arguments clearly showed that the anti-imperialists had abandoned the
natural-rights philosophy of the Declaration of Independence for a complicated
Darwinian view of the world. According to this view, which appeared to be
substantiated by the science of the day and by the writings of historians like
Herbert Baxter Adams, geography, race, and political institutions were
inextricably intertwined. The temperate zone—specifically the northern part of
it—bred the "Germanic" race, from which Americans were descended. Free
institutions were associated with the rise of that race; a study of other cultures
showed no similar institutions. Because they alone were capable of using
liberty wisely, the Germans had already risen to a cultural level far beyond that
of any other race and were possibly destined to supplant all others. In view of
their inability to survive in the tropics, however, it was not quite clear how this
was to be accomplished; and for that reason, perhaps, the anti-imperialists
preferred to see the Anglo-Saxons stay at home, in their native habitat. In any
case, to mingle their blood with that of Asiatics would be a fatal departure from
what Charles Francis Adams, for example, called the "cardinal principle in our
policy as a race." He referred to our Indian policy, which he admitted had
been harsh; but it had "saved the Anglo-Saxon stock from being a nation of
half-breeds." The acquisition of the Philippines would again endanger the
purity of the old stock, on which America's very survival depended.

An examination of the arguments against annexation of the Philippines leads
to a number of interesting conclusions. In the first place, it is difficult, after
having read their writings and speeches to convince oneself that the
anti-imperialists had the better of the argument, as historians have tended to
assume. Whatever the merits of the expansionists' contention that the Filipinos
were not ready for self-government, the expansionists were at least consistent in
the conclusions which they drew from it. If it was true that the Filipinos could not
govern themselves, the humane policy (although not necessarily the wisest one)

was to govern them ourselves. The anti-imperialists, on the other hand, while sharing the expansionists' basic assumption (an assumption contrary to the spirit of American democracy), were perfectly willing to leave the Filipinos to their fate—certainly a most un-Christian policy if they were indeed unable to manage their own affairs. So far as the moral argument had any validity at all, the anti-imperialists were on weak ground; and since they insisted on treating the question as a matter of right and wrong, it seems fair to judge them accordingly.

But it is not possible to condemn anti-imperialists for holding certain opinions on race unless one is willing to condemn the entire society of which they were a part. The fact is that the atmosphere of the late nineteenth century was so thoroughly permeated with racist thought (reinforced by Darwinism) that few men managed to escape it. The idea that certain cultures and races were naturally inferior to others was almost universally held by educated, middle-class, respectable Americans—in other words, by the dominant majority. The widespread and almost unconscious adherence to it was unmistakably manifested, in the same period, in the national policy toward minorities more familiar to American experience than the Filipinos, and in particular toward immigrants and Negroes. This was the period of the first serious restrictions on immigration; it was the period of the South's successful re-elimination of the Negro from white society. Men who called themselves liberals—survivors of the antislavery crusade and the battles of the sixties and seventies on behalf of the Negroes: liberal Republicans, mugwumps, "independents"—acquiesced in these developments. A study of anti-imperialism makes it a little clearer why they did, for the anti-imperialist movement was dominated by these same men—men like Schurz, Adams, Jordan, and Moorfield Storey. Except for Storey, these men had now receded from their earlier idealism. They continued to speak of their part in the struggle for Negro rights, to refer to it with pride, but by referring to it as a fight which had already been won they indicated their indifference to the continuing plight of the Southern Negro. Indeed, they had abandoned him, as they now proposed to abandon the Filipinos. They had no further interest in crusading; the times, it appeared, called for retrenchment.

twelve anti-imperialists and imperialists compared: racism and economic expansion

RICHARD E. WELCH, JR.

Richard Welch (b. 1924) of Lafayette College challenges Lasch's interpretation and McCormick's assumption in 1962 that the imperialists and anti-imperialists were both economic expansionists who simply differed over means. Welch finds the questions complex, and he makes distinctions between notions of racial superiority and racial subjugation, and economic expansion and economic domination. He agrees with those historians who argue that the decade of the 1890s was a major turning point in American foreign relations. Besides numerous scholarly articles on the anti-imperialists, Professor Welch has published a political biography of one of the most vociferous anti-imperialist leaders, Senator George F. Hoar of Massachusetts (George Frisbie Hoar and the Half-Breed Republicans [1971]).

Source: Richard E. Welch, Jr., "Motives and Objectives of Anti-Imperialists, 1898," *Mid-America* 51 (April 1969): 119–29. Used by permission of the publisher.

For American historians writing in the 1930's and 1940's, the anti-imperialists of 1898 were good men if unfortunately ineffectual. With the 1950's there was an increasing tendency to underscore their lack of understanding of power politics and their inability to offer satisfactory policy alternatives, but the anti-imperialists remained high-minded and sincere. Over the last decade their high-mindedness has been questioned and the sincerity of their anti-imperialism has been challenged. They have been charged with being as racist and as expansionist as their opponents and rather more selfish and hypocritical. Certain recent authors have emphasized the Anglo-Saxon intolerance of the anti-imperialists and have implied that their opposition to colonial annexation was not the result of a concern for the Filipino but of a dread of being contaminated by him. Other authors have emphasized the desire of the anti-imperialists to see the economic dominion of America extended and have implied that their opposition to colonial annexation was not the result of a belief in the principle of self-determination but of a conviction that economic imperialism would proceed more safely and smoothly if unburdened by the tasks of colonial administration.

This essay will seek to prove that the "racism" of many of the anti-imperialists was of a very different kind and degree than that of their opponents and the policy objectives of most anti-imperialists appreciably different from those of the expansionists. The Great Debate of 1898 was not an idle bit of shadow-boxing between like-minded Social Darwinists who quarreled only over the degree to which American imperialism should be camouflaged.

The central difficulty in any effort to characterize the motives and objectives of the anti-imperialists is obviously one of identification. All students of the anti-imperialist movement would probably agree that its membership was characterized by diversity and heterogeneity. Consequently, it is possible to find in that membership at least a few spokesmen for almost any aim or motive. Any movement that encompassed William Jennings Bryan and Andrew Carnegie would appear to invite historiographical dispute.

Certainly there is a lengthy slate of candidates available to one who would seek to offer a list of "representative anti-imperialists"—men who represent the majority weight as well as the diversity of the movement. From an initial list of fifty persons, the author has selected twenty-five whom he believes as "representative" in their influence and views, their motives and objectives as any like number that might be selected. In alphabetical order they are: Charles Francis Adams, Jr.; Edward Atkinson; George S. Boutwell; Samuel Bowles, Jr.; Gamaliel Bradford; William Jennings Bryan; Andrew Carnegie; Grover Cleveland; George F. Edmunds; Edwin L. Godkin; Arthur Pue Gorman; Thomas Wentworth Higginson; George F. Hoar; William James; David Starr Jordan; George C. Mercer; Richard Olney; Thomas B. Reed; Carl Schurz; Edwin Burritt Smith; Moorfield Storey; George G. Vest; Winslow Warren; Herbert Welsh; and Erving Winslow.* Assuming that these twenty-five men

---

* The author's initial list embraced an additional twenty-five names: Augustus O. Bacon; Donelson Caffery; John Carlisle; John Jay Chapman; Bourke Cochran; Patrick Collins; William A. Croffut; Theodore Ledyard Cuyler; Finley Peter Dunne; William C. Endicott; William Lloyd Garrison, Jr.; Edward Everett Hale; Eugene Hale; Benjamin Harrison; John B. Henderson; Josephine Shaw Lowell; Charles Eliot Norton; Patrick O'Farrell;

fairly represent the weight as well as the breadth of the leadership of the
anti-imperialist movement, what conclusions can be drawn respecting the
more typical motives and policy objectives of that leadership?

There is little profit in belaboring the fact that this group incorporates a
diversity of motives. There were obvious distinctions in the fears and hopes
that determined their respective decisions to denounce the acquisition of a
colonial empire at the conclusion of the Spanish-American War. If William
James worried over the traditional values and unique mission of America,
George Vest confined his attention primarily to questions of legality, while
Edward Atkinson emphasized the economic and military dangers embodied
in a policy of colonialism. All of these anti-imperialists shared the common
characteristic that it was primarily their fears that dictated their opposition to
a policy of colonial acquisition, but the nature of their apprehensions varied.
If some feared for the principles of the Declaration of Independence, others
feared for the national debt, the Monroe Doctrine, the letter of the Constitution,
the tradition of civilian rule, the international reputation of the country,
the lives of America's sons, the diplomatic independence of the Republic,
or the political prospects of the Democratic Party. Obviously certain
of these fears were more "high-minded" than others, but on balance were
they inspired by a principled opposition to injustice or a selfish concern for
personal advantage and racial purity?

No one of these men determined to oppose imperialism *primarily* on the
grounds that such opposition would work to his personal or political
advantage, and only in one case—that of Arthur Pue Gorman—is it probable
that partisan animosity played a determining role. Cleveland, Olney, and
Bryan were strong party men, but it was not primarily on the ground of
partisan advantage that they opposed the colonial policy of the McKinley
Administration. But if it was not personal or partisan advantage that inspired
these men, was it racism? Is it true that "the anti-imperialists were in fact no
more Jeffersonian in their essential outlook" than their opponents and shared to
the full the conviction of the expansionists in "the natural inequality of
men"? . . .

Judged by the standards of today, no participant in the Philippines Debate
was a cultural relativist, far less a "Soul Brother." It is furthermore true that
certain of the anti-imperialists, and particularly those from the South, were
as firmly convinced of the inferiority and incapacity of colored races as the
most vociferous exponent of the "White Man's Burden." But is it true that
it was an antipathy to "inferior races" that primarily determined the
position of the anti-imperialists and is it true that the emphasis of the
anti-imperialists on the "differentness" of the Malay is a true indication
of racism as that term is to be defined in the context of the 1890's?

Gorman, Bryan, Vest, Jordan, Carnegie, and Godkin were white supremacists

Albert S. Parsons; Henry Codman Potter; Henry Wade Rogers; John Sherman;
William Graham Sumner; Mark Twain; John Sharp Williams. Each of these names was
dropped from the final list in the belief that the motivation and aims of the person in
question were either less certain or less influential than those of their compatriots or merely
repetitive.

in their separate ways and degrees; Schurz spoke dourly of passions "bred by the tropical sun"; and even Charles Francis Adams, Jr., spoke deprecatingly of half-breed peoples and made occasional reference to "the Barbarian and the Heathen," but a number of the leading anti-imperialists, and in particular men such as Storey, Hoar, Higginson, Atkinson, Boutwell, Warren, Welsh, and James, can only be labeled "racist" by straining definition past utility and imposing upon one generation the social experience and emotional guilt of another.

Surely there was an element of *noblesse oblige* in the attitude of Storey and Hoar towards the Filipino. Both believed that the most fortunate of mortals were those who had been born into the world not only as white Anglo-Saxons but as descendants of the heroes of Lexington and Concord. These men, however, were the recipients of the praise and gratitude of Felipe Agoncillo and each man in turn proclaimed Emilio Aguinaldo to be the George Washington of the Pacific. Hoar, the chosen adviser of the Filipino exile committee in London, did not categorize peoples by the classification of Social Darwinism. With Storey, Atkinson, Warren, and a dozen other leading anti-imperialists, he was convinced that the Filipinos were civilized, capable, and Christian. They had established an orderly civil administration that enjoyed general support and they possessed—as did any organized society—the inherent right of national self-determination.

Before charging the anti-imperialist leadership as a whole with racism, one should at least pause to evaluate the conviction of many of these men that in fighting imperialism they were fighting again the crusade of their youth against slavery, and evaluate as well their record in various "civil rights" causes. Adams, Atkinson, Boutwell, Bradford, Edmunds, Higginson, Hoar, and Schurz had all been active participants in the anti-slavery crusade of the 1850's, had without exception cheered the enlargement of the Civil War into a war for freedom as well as union, and, again without exception, had supported the initial purposes and acts of Radical Reconstruction. The same could be said of the fathers of Samuel Bowles, Moorfield Storey, Winslow Warren, and Erving Winslow. In the decade of the 1890's some of these men were still associated with the support of the Freedman and the protection of his political rights, nor would this association end in all cases with that decade. As Hoar and Edmunds had sought in 1890 to pass a Federal Elections bill and render effective the Fifteenth Amendment, Moorfield Storey accepted election as first president of the N.A.A.C.P. in 1911.

The chief point to be made, however, is that though many of these men expressed a strong antipathy to the idea of "tropical races" being incorporated in the American Republic and made endless references to the inability of the Malay to understand the values and institutions of that Republic, there is a valid distinction to be made between their views respecting "racial difference" and those of their imperialist opponents. If the anti-imperialists were victims of the belief that the white man was by nature the most capable and intelligent and the most able to benefit from liberty and self-government, a majority of them did not believe that other races were inherently incapable and unintelligent or automatically disabled from enjoying the benefits of liberty and self-government. Carl Schurz did not believe that the Filipinos could establish a government in the Anglo-Saxon mould, but he was convinced that they should be allowed the right to establish a government in the mould they desired. Charles Francis Adams, Jr., and William James scoffed at the notion that the United States had a divine mission to uplift and improve "our little brown brothers," but their scorn was largely inspired by a belief that the United States had shamefully mistreated the minority groups who resided within its continental limits and the island natives would best be served by being allowed to develop . . . a national life along their own lines, unhindered by the humanitarian interference or self-seeking ambitions of America.

There is a legitimate distinction to be drawn between the ideas of race difference possessed by a James or Adams and the master race notions and Social Darwinian concepts of a Mahan or Roosevelt. And this distinction holds for a good majority of the anti-imperialist leadership. If many of them were infected by racial snobbery, few suffered the virus of racial domination; if they did not want the Filipino as a fellow citizen, neither did they wish him as a vassal. Erving Winslow thought no people so worthy as those of "old New England stock," but he wished the Filipino free and he wished him well in his own national self-development. Surely the Filipino leaders of the time drew a clear distinction between their American friends and foes and attributed to the former a degree of sympathy and understanding sharply at variance to that of the supporters of the colonial policy of William McKinley. To say they exaggerated this difference is not to deny its existence.

Was there also a significant difference between the policy objectives of the anti-imperialists and their opponents, or is Professor Thomas J. McCormick correct in his declaration that expansionist ambitions characterized both sides in the Philippines Debate? In Professor McCormick's words, "anti-imperialists and imperialists alike, though differing over the techniques to be employed, favored a militant American expansion into world markets," and the debate they waged was "a relatively secondary one, centering upon means, not ends."*

Can the twenty-five men listed above properly be labeled, "non-colonial

---

* Thomas J. McCormick, "A Commentary on The Anti-Imperialists and Twentieth-Century Foreign Policy," *Studies on the Left,* III (1962), 28–33. McCormick argues further that there was "a general consensus among the 'power elite' of the day on the primacy of industrial overproduction as the cause of America's social-economic ills, and agreement upon economic expansion abroad as the chief means of overcoming economic stagnation and social catastrophe." Within that "power elite" he would presumably place the bulk of the anti-imperialist leadership: ". . . the Anti-Imperialists . . . were dedicated to the rapid expansion of the American economic system abroad as the chief way out of the stagnation and social upheaval of the 1890's." (p. 29) McCormick's "Commentary" is addressed in part to an interesting if rather confusing paper by John W. Rollins. Professor Rollins sees the anti-imperialists as advocates of "the ideology of laissez faire liberalism"; the latter he considers the "framework for an expanding industrial system," the rationale of this country's effort to "get on with the peaceful conquest of the world," and the essential "legacy of the Anti-Imperialists" to the twentieth century; John W. Rollins, "The Anti-Imperialists and the Twentieth-Century American Foreign Policy," *Studies on the Left,* III (1962), 9–24. Another commentary on Rollins' paper, by Professor Harold Baron, criticizes the anti-imperialists for their "failure to link imperialism with the foundation of capitalist society" and to see the connection between industrial monopolies and imperialism, but for Baron the anti-imperialists are economic dolts not economic imperialists; *ibid.,* 24–27.

expansionists," subtle advocates of *"Imperium in anti-imperio!"*? Was their quarrel with the foreign policy of the McKinley Administration simply an argument over means, waged by men who possessed in common with their opponents a determination to expand the industrial markets and economic influence of America throughout the globe?

Of these twenty-five men, no more than four could be classified as advocates of economic imperialism, if by that term one implies the advocacy of governmental pressures in behalf of trade expansion. A majority of them were advocates of free trade and an even larger majority saw a connection between the domestic tranquility of the nation and the prosperity of all sectors of its economy, but only Atkinson, Carnegie, Jordan, and Olney gave even sporadic allegiance to diplomatic intervention in behalf of the expansion of American industrial markets. On balance the anti-imperialist leadership had no more use for dollar diplomacy than for gunboat diplomacy. They favored the expansion of trade, but they opposed either governmental coercion or colonial acquisition as instruments for its promotion. Certainly several of them were convinced that the United States, about to outstrip Britain as the most industrially productive nation in the world, would enjoy increasing benefit from the natural operations of international trade and its "law" of comparative advantage, but to say this is not to offer support for the current historiographical fashion which would minimize the difference in objectives between the anti-imperialists and their opponents. The anti-imperialists believed, on balance, that it was immoral and dangerous for the Republic to acquire distant and heavily populated territories that would remain by design in a stage of perpetual colonial subservience. They believed that whether the nation's flag should follow the nation's trade was a question of marked relevance to the safety of that Republic.

When these anti-imperialists offered economic arguments in behalf of their position they were arguments against the economic costs of militarism and the economic dislocations occasioned by tax-free colonial imports and an expensive colonial bureaucracy. Only a minority of these anti-imperialists placed any great emphasis on economic considerations, in any case. It was not the level of the national debt that concerned the majority but rather the nation's philosophical consistency, social homogeneity, and world image.

Those who articulated most clearly the economic arguments against colonialism were, interestingly enough, usually members of the Republican minority within the anti-imperialist ranks. Carnegie, Edmunds, Reed, and Hoar, together with the mugwumpish Atkinson, were the men most likely to stress the economic dangers embodied in a policy of imperialism. All were men who wished to see the expansion of American trade and the sale of surplus production in foreign markets; none believed that it was either right or economically necessary that American goods be "exported at the cannon's mouth." Three of these men, Edmunds, Reed, and Hoar, were not only staunch Republicans but professional politicians. Edmunds had retired from Congress in 1891 and Reed would follow in the summer of 1899, but with Hoar they had been exponents in the 1880's of the political ideology and practice of the Half-Breed Republicans. It is in the self-contradictory aims and ambitions of Half-Breed Republicanism that one can discover the key to the substantive difference in the economic objectives of such men as Edmunds and Hoar as contrasted to those of such younger men as Albert Beveridge and Henry Cabot Lodge.

As a separate faction within the Republican party, the Half-Breeds are distinguishable only in the late 1870's and 1880's, but the political creed of the Half-Breeds had a longer life, serving indeed as the ideological bridge between the Republican party of Ulysses S. Grant and that of Theodore Roosevelt. This creed incorporated aspirations for the American economy both abroad and at home. The Half-Breeds identified the future of their country with its industrial strength. They desired the protection and diversification of industry, an improved standard of living for the American workingman, a national banking and currency system suitable to the needs and safety of American business, and the expansion of foreign markets. For the most part they were too economy-minded to favor large military expenditures and, with some exceptions, they had little use for jingoism and diplomatic belligerence. Economic expansion was rightful and necessary, but it should be the peaceful accomplishment of private enterprise. Business and Politics were equal partners in the economic and social progress of America, and it was a dangerous politician who by a rambunctious diplomacy would endanger our separation from the embroilments of Europe and so risk disturbing the natural expansion of the American industrial economy.

Such Republicans as Hoar, Edmunds, and Reed had believed this in 1880; so, too, they, and others such as Justin Morrill and Eugene Hale, believed it in 1898. Whatever the economic logic of their position at either date, it was a position clearly distinguished from either the "Large Policy" of Mahan and Roosevelt or the dream of imperial spoils of Albert Beveridge and Whitelaw Reid. The two Republican senators from Massachusetts—George F. Hoar and Henry Cabot Lodge—viewed the association between the expansion of the nation's trade and the expansion of the nation's diplomatic responsibilities in a very different light. The two Republican senators from Maine—Eugene Hale and William P. Frye—held very different notions respecting the economic requirements and priorities of the Republic.

The economic expansion envisioned by those former Half-Breed Republicans who joined the ranks of anti-imperialism was an expansion that would peacefully and indeed automatically follow the accelerating growth and excellence of America's manufactured product. To call men such as George F. Hoar "non-colonial imperialists" is to give imperialism a definition so broad that few statesmen of 19th Century America would escape inclusion. If all but the more extreme economic nationalists are to be charged with a desire for imperial dominion, one must discover new terms with which to describe the debate over colonial expansion which followed the Spanish-American War.

That debate possessed substance as well as rhetoric. Not only is there a valid distinction to be drawn between the racial attitudes and orientation of many of the anti-imperialists and their opponents, but their policy objectives and economic ambitions were never identical and at points clearly opposed to those of the expansionists.

Professors Lasch, Williams, and McCormick and their followers have put us in their debt by demanding that we re-assess the evidence of the Philippines Debate and evaluate again the motives and policy objectives of its participants. Such a re-assessment, however, need not produce the conclusion that the debate was only an exhibition of shadow-boxing between like-minded expansionists whose quarrel was confined to differences of tactics, nor the conclusion that the debate was one characterized by an equal display of parochial selfishness and racial intolerance on both sides. One may conclude to the contrary that the Philippines Debate of 1898 was fought over certain of the more basic and continuing questions of American foreign policy, and contested by men whose assumptions of the essential nature and mission of the American Republic were significantly different. If never to be repeated with the same ingredients, that debate remains a respectable subject of study, relevant to the concerns of the present generation of Americans and its historians.

thirteen
anti-imperialism in the philippines: the filipino plea for independence

TEODORO A. AGONCILLO

By January 1899, when Emilio Aguinaldo established a new Filipino government at Malolos, the United States and Spain had signed the Treaty of Paris annexing the Philippines to America. Aguinaldo had been transported from Hong Kong to his country on the American gunboat McCulloch *at the start of the Spanish-American War, and he believed that American officials had promised that if he helped to defeat the Spanish, his nation would realize independence. In February 1899, war broke out between Filipino and American soldiers. Teodoro A. Agoncillo (b. 1912), trained in the American-introduced Filipino public schools, and now professor of history at the University of the Philippines, has written a number of studies on the Filipino side of the story, including* The Revolt of the Masses *(1956) and, with Oscar Alfonso,* History of the Filipino People *(1967). The following selection from* Malolos: The Crisis of the Republic *reveals Agoncillo's sympathy for the Filipino anti-imperialists who were defeated in a bloody war with occupying American forces.*

Source: Teodoro A. Agoncillo, *Malolos: The Crisis of the Republic* (Quezon City, Philippines: University of the Philippines Press, 1960), pp. 311, 315–16, 322–25, 355–58, 362–65, 372, 429–34, 450–52, 532–36. Used by permission of the author.

As early as June 10, 1898, [Felipe] Agoncillo* wrote Aguinaldo that a representative be sent to the United States in order to ascertain American intentions regarding the Philippines. Owing perhaps to this suggestion, the decree of June 23 provided for the creation of a committee to take charge of what may properly be called a propaganda corps. On August 7, Aguinaldo instructed Agoncillo to publish the "Act of Proclamation" and the "Manifesto to Foreign Governments" in the Hong Kong papers. Furthermore, he exhorted Agoncillo to exert all efforts in publicizing the Philippine situation, adding:

> *It is important that you should go [to the United States] as soon as possible, so that McKinley's Government would know the true situation. Show him that our people have their own Government, civil organizations in the provinces already exist, and soon the Congress of Representatives of these provinces will meet. Tell him that they cannot do with the Philippines what they like. . . . * * * The policy that you will pursue in the United States is as follows: make them understand that whatever might be their intentions toward us it will not be possible for them to overrule the sentiments of the people represented by the government and so it cannot be ignored by them. . . . Still, do not accept any contracts or give any promises respecting protection or annexation, because we shall see first if we can obtain independence. That is what we shall secure in the meantime, if it should be possible to do so. * * * Give them to understand in a way that you are unable to obligate yourself, but once we are independent then we shall be able to make arrangements with them.*

*　*　*

In what may be regarded as final instructions to Agoncillo, Aguinaldo, on August 30, wrote:

> *It is said that General Merritt is going away to take part in the work of the Commission [Paris Peace Conference.] On this account, it is important that you proceed as quickly as possible to America, in order to know what will take place. If perchance we should go back to Spanish control, ask them [the Americans] to help us as the French helped them during their own revolution and ask also the terms. * * * I am not informed if it is true that our representatives will be admitted to the Commission; if they should be admitted go immediately to the place where they will meet, which is said here to be in Paris, September 15, and if among our countrymen there or in London there be one who will agree with the policy of the government, according to your instructions, propose his name at once so that credentials may be sent him. * * * In whatever agreement you will make you will insert as a condition the recognition of this government.*

* Aide to Aguinaldo.

At almost the same time, Aguinaldo instructed the diplomatic representatives abroad to entangle the United States in the affairs of the Philippines so that she might be forced to prevent foreign Powers from dividing up the country. . . .

The ship docked in San Francisco on September 22. Since it had been known in the United States and in Europe that Agoncillo left Hong Kong on his way to America, the Americans, in their staggering ignorance of geography, expected that he would arrive on civilized American soil naked, except for the G-strings. They were, however, dumbfounded to see a highly educated man, complete with hat and well-pressed European suit, go down the gangplank with superior airs. On the same day, he and [General Francis V.] Greene took the train for Washington, D.C., where they arrived on September 27. It was during this land journey to the American capital that Agoncillo learned from the newspapers that he would not be officially received by Washington. He then requested Greene to make arrangements with President McKinley in order to confer with him officially. Greene, an understanding and accommodating man, did so upon their arrival in Washington, but the President expressed his regret that he could not see Agoncillo officially because it would be contrary to American understanding with Spain. However, he expressed his willingness to see Agoncillo unofficially. Disappointed, Agoncillo then sounded out the State Department regarding the acceptance of his credentials. He was met with a rebuff. At this point, he took it upon himself to see President McKinley at 10:00 A.M. of October 1. He was politely received in the official reception room. Agoncillo recounted to McKinley the Filipinos' struggles to be free. Although the President listened politely it was obvious that Agoncillo's mission to the United States was bound to fail. He then asked McKinley if he would be allowed to state the aims and purposes of the Philippine Government. McKinley answered that a secret note to this effect should be handed to him, a note, McKinley added, that should be personal and without Agoncillo's official designation. On October 3, Agoncillo handed the note to Assistant Secretary of State Adee, who in turn showed it to the President. The latter instructed Adee to accept Agoncillo's note on condition that he would agree to some amendments. Agoncillo, after conferring with Adee and learning that insistence on acceptance of his official note might result in its total rejection, gracefully accepted the amendments. The note, in its final form, reviewed the background of the Filipino-American relations, and then continued:

6. *The lawful government of the natives now functioning in the Philippine Islands has been sanctioned by the only legitimate source of public power, the vote of its fellow-citizens, whose authority and representation it has, and it has in fact been recognized, not objected to, and utilized by the American nation. Said Government, in the performance of its duties, considers that it must address itself to the American public powers and remind them of its right, owing to its existence, its services, and its loyalty, to be consulted and considered and given a voice and decisive vote in all the questions to be finally settled in the Paris Conference or in consequence thereof, concerning the Philippines.*

7. *The present lawful Philippine Government of which the invincible leader General Emilio Aguinaldo is the president, also believes that the moment has come to remind and even notify, if proper, in a formal and precise manner, the Illustrious President and Government of Washington of its existence and normal and regular functioning, as well as of its relations of reciprocity with the authorities of the American Republic in the Philippine Islands.*

8. *It desires to state (in the same manner), that the Philippine people unanimously confirms its independence and confides that the American people will recognize the same, mindful of the offers made and obligations contracted in its name, proclaiming the principles of liberty, justice and right expressed in its famous, sacred Declaration of Independence for the benefit of the new nation which logically rises in that part of the globe under the impulse of its present beneficent and humanitarian action.*

9. *And the Philippine people hope that pending a permanent understanding for the evacuation of their territory, their present lawful* de facto *government will be accorded the rights of a belligerent and such other rights as may be proper, in order to compel Spain to submit to the just historical law which deprives her of the tutelage she has arrogated to herself over those Islands and which she was incapable of carrying on humanely and socially without detriment to the general interests.*

10. *The Philippine people and their aforesaid Government and legitimate representatives pray and urge the noble President of the Republic of the United States of America and the public powers thereof to be guided by the aspirations, recognize the rights and sanctions, and proclaim, imbued by their sentiments of justice and honor, that which was offered by their international representatives, as set forth in this document.*

It was then agreed that Agoncillo's note be sent to the American commissioners in Paris. Agoncillo was further advised to hurry thither in order to have an interview with the commissioners. It is apparent that official Washington wanted to get rid of him in order to free itself from the possible embarrassment of dealing with the representative of the Philippine Government that the United States had no intention of recognizing. But Agoncillo thought that such show of assumed or studied sympathy was an invitation for the Philippines to send a representative to the Commission in Paris. While he thought that many Americans were for Philippine independence, yet Agoncillo clearly saw that he was fighting a lost cause and warned Aguinaldo that the people should be prepared for a possible conflict with the Americans. . . .

The deliberations of the commissioners were closely followed by the Filipino agents abroad, particularly by Agoncillo, whose duty it was to present before the conference the Filipino side of the Philippine question. As the deliberations dragged on and Agoncillo was not given a chance to air his views, the agents in Europe and in Hong Kong came to the conclusion that there was nothing more to do than to wait for developments. Agoncillo, however, upon learning of the conclusion of the treaty, submitted a memorandum to the Peace Commissioners, through General Greene, in which he said that the treaty "cannot be accepted as binding by my government inasmuch as the commission did not hear the Filipino people or admit them into its deliberations, when they have the undisputable right to intervene in all that might affect their future life." The commission merely shrugged its shoulders and ignored Agoncillo's protest. Agoncillo, as early as December 1, had admitted that the Philippines would be annexed to the United States. In view of Agoncillo's failure to be heard in the Paris conference, Ramon Abarca, treasurer of the Filipino Republican Committee of Paris, telegraphed Apacible on December 14 proposing the immediate return of Agoncillo to Washington. It was felt that Agoncillo's only hope was in preventing the ratification of the treaty by the American Senate.

At the point when all seemed lost and when the Filipino leaders sensed the inevitability of an armed conflict with the Americans, they proposed a Filipino-Spanish alliance in order to fight the new enemy. The weakness of Spain's economy and international position, what with the war in Cuba sapping her resources and the reluctance of the European concert to intervene in Cuban affairs on behalf of Spain, obviously encouraged the Filipino leaders to take advantage of the situation to force Spain to deal with them directly. Most of Luzon was in the hands of the rebels; the Visayas was seething; and the Spanish forces in Mindanao were floundering helplessly with no hope of aid either from Manila or from Spain. With thousands of Spaniards taken prisoner, the rebel leaders tried to strengthen their bargaining power by using the Spanish prisoners as bait. Consequently, they advanced the following propositions as *modus vivendi*: (1) the conclusion of an agreement of peace and friendship between the Philippines and Spain as soon as the Philippines was recognized; (2) the renunciation by the Philippines and Spain of any claim to public and private property; (3) the grant to Spain of the most-favored nation right; (4) the payment of ₱7,000,000 to the Philippine Government; (5) the cession to the Philippines of the Carolines and the Marianas; (6) the prohibition by Spain for the friars to go to the Philippines; and (7) the renunciation by the Spanish friars of all claims to property in the Philippines and their departure from the country within forty-five days. Evidently, none of the Spaniards took the propositions seriously.

Aguinaldo, realizing the hopelessness of fighting for the recognition of an independent Philippines, now appealed to McKinley, proposing (1) that the Spanish possessions in Oceania be formed into a state and named "Republic of the Philippines" under the protection of the United States; (2) that the purpose of the protectorate under the United States was to make Spain abandon her possessions in Oceania and, too, to make the United States work for the recognition of the Republic by the foreign Powers; (3) that a commission composed of Filipinos and Americans be created to determine the period of protectorate and to formulate a treaty of alliance between the Philippines and the United States. McKinley, however, had no need for such an ambitious alliance, for he had already made up his mind that the Philippines should belong to the United States.

* * *

What is probably his best brief in support of the Filipino contention is contained in his *Memorial to the Senate*. Here, then, is Agoncillo holding his brief against the action of the United States in ignoring the independence aspirations of the Filipinos:

> *I cannot believe that in any possible action on the part of the American republic towards my country there is an intent to ignore, as to the ten millions of human beings I represent, the right the free government of America preserves to the lowliest of her inhabitants; but rather prefer to think that in the rush of arms this right for a moment may have been obscured in the minds of some of America's liberty-loving and enlightened citizens.*
>
> *I have taken occasion in a communication to the Secretary of State to point out that by the rule of international law, maintained without exception by the American Government, the Philippine Republic has been for many months entitled to national recognition, possessing, as it has, since June, 1898, a government both de facto and de jure, capable of enforcing its laws at home, or carrying out its undertakings with foreign Governments, and of maintaining itself against Spain.*
>
> *Before the appointment of the peace commissioners on September 12, 1898, American officials had fully recognized and had communicated to their Government the fact that it was no longer possible for Spain, under any circumstances, to regain possession of the Philippines; a point most essential to be considered in determining whether a new, independent nation should be recognized.*
>
> *In a memorandum concerning the Philippine Islands, made on August 27, 1898, by General F. V. Greene he states:*
>
> *"The Spanish Government is completely demoralized, and Spanish power is dead, beyond the possibility of resurrection. Spain would be unable to govern these islands if we surrender them."*
>
> *From the foregoing, it must appear that the Philippine nation had achieved its independence free from any danger of losing it at the hands of the Spaniards, prior even to the signing of the protocol. This is shown by the Executive Document No. 62, now before the Senate, which document contains much testimony concerning the productive capacity of the Philippine Islands, and their mineral and agricultural wealth, but little evidence touching the probability of maintaining the American government in these islands irrespective of the desires of their people, and no direct testimony that the American Government had known from the beginning that the Filipinos were struggling for independence and with success, and including copies*

*of the declaration of independence of the Philippine Republic and of
the laws passed pursuant thereto, and showing that the Government
knew that there was in existence a regularly organized and constituted
republican government controlling the Islands and having General
Aguinaldo at its head.*

*I have already alluded to the fact that Spain had no power to
deliver possession to the United States of the Philippine Islands,
having been driven from these islands by just wrath of their
inhabitants; and by way of illustration of this point, I venture
to file herewith a map of the Philippine Archipelago, designating the
principal islands under the control of the respective nations, and showing
that America is in actual possession at this time of one hundred and
forty three square miles of territory, with a population of three
hundred thousand, while the Philippine Government is in possession
and control of 167,845 square miles, with a population of 9,395,000,
and only a few scattered garrisons are to be found in islands having
an area of 51,693 square miles, with a population of 305,000. The
figures as to the Spanish possession should be diminished, and those
of the Philippine Government enlarged by virtue of the fact that
the inhabitants of the islands where Spanish troops yet remain have
practically confined such troops to the narrow quarters of their
garrison towns.*

*Spain, therefore, having been driven away, as I have stated, and
the inhabitants having established a government satisfactory to
themselves and maintaining order throughout the territories under its
control, what justification can any other nation advance for interfering
with my country or refusing to extend toward it the obligations of
international law? Could Spain give to any nation a better right
than she possessed? She could not confer possession, for she did not
enjoy it, and any foreign right of possession claimed by her had been
extinguished by the destruction of her sovereignty over my country.
She could not create by treaty or otherwise, as against the Philippine
Islands, any right, except it be the right to conquer them, and if
such right be claimed, it exists not because of cession on the part of
Spain, but because of its own inherent force, and must be as
powerful on behalf of any other nations as it is on behalf of the
United States. If, therefore, America claims the right to make war upon
my countrymen for the purpose of conquering them, and thus destroying
another republic, so equally may Germany, France, and England, or
any other powerful nation, claim the same right.*

* * *

The news of the annexation of the Philippines to the United States
was received in the country with mixed feeling. To the vested interests, the
Treaty of Paris was a wish fulfilled; to the idealistic patriots and nationalists,
the news was the harbinger of dark days to come. In Pasig, the residents

passed a resolution expressing their loyalty to the Philippine Government and to Aguinaldo and offering their lives in the interest of the country's freedom. Resolutions protesting the annexation of the Philippines to the United States were passed by the residents of Navotas, Pateros, San Pedro Makati, San Felipe Neri, then in Manila Province; by the people of Ilocos Sur, Batanes, Tayabas, Albay, Camarines, Zambales, Samar, Ilocos Norte, Cagayan, Cavite, Pampanga, Capiz, Pangasinan, and other places such as Malibay (now in Pasay), Sampaloc, San Mateo, Las Piñas, Antipolo, San Miguel (Manila), Tondo, and Kalumpit. It was obvious that the people, as distinguished from the intelligentsia and the wealthy, were for continuing the struggle for freedom and independence. . . .

Much has been made out of the alleged chaotic condition into which the countryside and the Malolos Government itself had fallen. It had been the American opinion in Manila that the second half of 1898 was a period that might be characterized as "something akin to anarchy." This opinion was held by the Americans of the imperialist type, such as Dean C. Worcester. It led to more misunderstandings between the Filipinos and the Americans and resulted in increased tension. Such opinions as were held by the more unprejudiced Americans as W. B. Wilcox and L. R. Sargent, who conducted a survey of existing conditions of northern Luzon in the second half of 1898, unfortunately did not reach the Filipino leaders and the masses. Yet their findings are important as throwing light on the actual conditions and the range of authority exercised by the Malolos Government. Thus Sargent:

> I can state unreservedly, however, that Mr. Wilcox and I found the existing conditions to be much at variance with this opinion. During our absence from Manila we traveled more than six hundred miles in a very comprehensive circuit through the northern part of the island of Luzon, traversing a characteristic and important district. In this way we visited seven provinces, of which some were under the immediate control of the central government at Malolos, while others were remotely situated, separated from each other and from the seat of government by natural divisions of land and accessible only by lengthy and arduous travel. As a tribute to the efficiency of Aguinaldo's government and to the law-abiding character of his subjects, I offer the fact that Mr. Wilcox and I pursued our journey to Manila with only the most pleasing recollections of the quiet and orderly life which we found the natives to be leading under the new regime.

Sargent then proceeded to tell of their pleasant trip to northern Luzon where they were royally dined and wined by the Filipinos and honored with presentations of Spanish plays. Concluding his estimate, Sargent said:

> I cannot see what better gage we can obtain at present of the intelligence and ambition of the whole Filipino race than the progress that has been made by its favored members with the limited

opportunities at their command. Throughout the island a thirst for knowledge is manifested, and an extravagant respect for those who possess it. * * * The heroes of this people are not heroes of war, but of science and invention. Without a rival, the American who is best known by reputation in Luzon is Mr. Edison and any native with the slightest pretension to education whom you may question on the subject will take delight in reciting a list of his achievements. The ruling Filipinos, during the existence of their provisional government, appreciated the necessity of providing public schools to be accessible to the poorer inhabitants. Had the events so shaped themselves as to have provided an opportunity for carrying into effect the plans formed on this point, it seems possible that the mental plane of the entire population might have been raised gradually to a surprising height.

A John Barrett, who argued for the retention of the Philippines on economic grounds, admitted that he had had a pleasant experience in his travels in the Philippines. Speaking of the Malolos Congress, he said:

By the middle of October, 1898, he [Aguinaldo] had assembled at Malolos a congress of one hundred men who would compare in behavior, manner, dress and education with the average men of the better classes of other Asiatic nations, possibly including the Japanese. These men, whose sessions I repeatedly attended, conducted themselves with great decorum, showed knowledge of debate and parliamentary law that would not compare unfavorably with the Japanese Parliament. The executive portion of the government was made up of a ministry of bright men who seemed to understand their respective positions. Each general division was subdivided with reference to practical work. There was a large force of under-secretaries and clerks, who appeared to be kept very busy with routine labor.

Even Consul Wildman,* realizing the unfairness of the common run of American opinion regarding the Filipinos and their government, officially warned the State Department of the futility of looking down upon the Filipino government and people with something akin to contempt. In a dispatch to John Basset Moore, Under-Secretary of State, he said:

. . . the Insurgent Government of the Philippine Islands cannot be dealt with as though they were North American Indians willing to be removed from one reservation to another at the whim of their masters. If the United States decides not to retain the Philippine Islands, its ten million people will demand independence, and the attempt of any foreign nation to obtain territory or coaling stations

* U.S. Consul at Hong Kong.

will be resisted with the same spirit with which they fought the
Spaniards.

The Filipino-American tension was not relieved by such professions of
honesty on the part of some Americans. What appeared triumphant at the
moment was the set opinions of the imperialists who looked upon the Filipinos
as charges to be educated and civilized. The tension increased when President
McKinley's Proclamation, which set forth for the first time the American
policy toward the Philippines, was published. [Major General Elwell] Otis
toned down the Proclamation in order to avoid exciting the Filipino leaders,
for the original Proclamation contained phrases such as "sovereignty,"
"right of cession" and others, which, it was feared, might be used by
Aguinaldo to incite the masses against the Americans. But General Miller, who
received a copy of the original Proclamation, published it in Iloilo on
January 4, 1899, and soon copies of this unedited version reached
Malolos. The Proclamation was at once subjected to a heavy barrage of verbal
fireworks, with Antonio Luna, the editor of the nationalistic *La Independencia,*
leading the attack. Luna pointed out that the policy enunciated in the
Proclamation was "merely a subterfuge to temporarily quiet the people until
measures could be inaugurated and applied to put in practice all the odious
features of government which Spain had employed" in the Philippines. On
January 5, 1899, Aguinaldo issued a peppery counter-proclamation which,
in effect, terminated the hitherto theoretical Filipino-American friendship. He
summarized the American importunities and violations of the ethics of
friendship, particularly the order to occupy Iloilo, and concluded:

Such procedures, so foreign to the dictates of culture and the usages
observed by civilized nations, gave me the right to act without
observing the usual rules of intercourse. Nevertheless, in order to
be correct to the end, I sent to General Otis commissioners charged
to solicit him to desist from his rash enterprise, but they were not
listened to.
My government can not remain indifferent in view of such a
violent and aggressive seizure of a portion of its territory by a nation
which arrogated to itself the title champion of oppressed nations.
Thus it is that my government is disposed to open hostilities if the
American troops attempt to take forcible possession of the Visayan
Islands. I denounce these acts before the world, in order that the
conscience of mankind may pronounce its infallible verdict as to who
are the true oppressors of nations and the tormentors of human kind.

Copies of this incendiary proclamation reached the masses and doubtless
incensed them at what they thought, rightly or wrongly, to be the American
perfidy. Aguinaldo himself must have realized its implications and promptly
ordered the recall of the copies left undistributed. In its place, another

proclamation was published in the *Heraldo de la Revolución* on the evening
of the same day. He said partly:

> *As in General Otis's proclamation he alluded to some instructions*
> *edited by His Excellency the President of the United States, referring*
> *to the administration of the matters in the Philippine Islands, I in*
> *the name of God, the root and fountain of all justice, and that of*
> *all the right which has been visibly granted to me to direct my dear*
> *brothers in the difficult work of our regeneration, protest most*
> *solemnly against this intrusion of the United States Government*
> *on the sovereignty of these islands.*
>
> *I equally protest in the name of the Filipino people against the*
> *said intrusion, because as they have granted their vote of confidence*
> *appointing me president of the nation, although I don't consider that*
> *I deserve such, therefore I consider it my duty to defend to death*
> *its liberty and independence.*

To Otis, the two proclamations were tantamount to a call to arms. He met
the situation by quietly taking precautionary measures. He strengthened
the American observation posts and alerted his troops. The result was an
apparent unconcern on his part and a dubious pacific intention on the part
of the protagonists. But the tense atmosphere could be felt, and the Filipinos
in and around Manila left for safer places. The exodus was so great that
"all avenues of exit were filled with vehicles" and the railroad cars filled
to capacity in transporting families to the north within the protective arm
of the Filipino army. It was estimated that some 40,000 inhabitants fled
"within a period of fifteen days." On the other hand, Aguinaldo's
proclamations had the effect of drawing the masses together, so much so
that some 20,000 Filipinos paraded at San Fernando, Pampanga, to show
their loyalty to their President. . . .

Tension between the Filipinos and the Americans increased and only a
slight incident was needed to break the relations completely. The Americans
charged the Filipino soldiers with entering deep into American territory
and with other alleged misdeeds calculated to break their relations. On
February 1, a detachment of American engineers was arrested by the Filipino
troops and sent to Malolos. The following day, Otis filed a protest with
Aguinaldo. The latter replied that the five Americans belonging to the Corps
of Engineers were merely detained and that they had already been released.
They were arrested, according to Aguinaldo, because they were well within
the Filipino lines on Solis Street, Tondo, and that the arrest was made
in accordance with the decree of October 20, 1898 prohibiting foreigners
from approaching the Filipino defensive works.

Misunderstanding continued. On February 2, General Arthur MacArthur
protested the presence of Colonel Luciano San Miguel's soldiers within his
territory. He wrote:

> *Sir: The line between my command and your command has been long*

established, and is well understood by yourself and myself.

It is quite necessary under present conditions that this line should not be passed by armed men of either command.

An armed party from your command now occupies the village in front of blockhouse No. 7, at a point considerably more than a hundred yards on my side of the line, and is very active in exhibiting hostile intentions. This party must be withdrawn to your side of the line at once.

From this date, if the line is crossed by your men with arms in their hands they must be regarded as subject to such action as I may deem necessary.

Colonel San Miguel wanted to avoid any conflict with the Americans and immediately wrote MacArthur::

My very dear Sir: In reply to yours, dated this day, in which you inform me that my soldiers have been passing the line of demarcation fixed by agreement, I desire to say that this is foreign to my wishes, and I shall give immediate orders in the premises that they retire.

San Miguel promptly wrote an order, in the presence of Major Strong, directing his officers at the outpost to withdraw from the American side of the line in question. Strong himself delivered the order to the Filipino officers in the outpost. The following day, February 3, the Filipino troops inside MacArthur's territory withdrew. The tension seemed to have been relaxed. The following night, February 4, a patrol of the Nebraska Regiment was detailed to the village of Santol, near the Balsaham (San Juan) Bridge. It was instructed not to allow Filipino soldiers to enter the village or its vicinity. All armed persons coming from the Filipino lines were to be ordered back and arrested if they refused. Only upon failure to arrest them should they be shot. At about eight o'clock in the evening, Private Willie W. Grayson with two other members of the Patrol advanced beyond the village to ascertain whether there were Filipino soldiers in the vicinity. Suddenly four armed men appeared before Grayson.

I yelled "halt" .... the man moved, I challenged with another "halt". Then he immediately shouted "Halto" to me. Well I thought the best thing to do was to shoot him. He dropped. Then two Filipinos sprang out of the gateway about fifteen feet from us. I called "Halt" and Miller fired and dropped one. I saw that another was left. Well I think I got my second Filipino that time. We retreated to where our six other fellows were and I said, "Line up fellows; the enemy are in here all through these yards." We then retreated to the pipe line and got behind the water work main and stayed there all night. It was some minutes after our second shots before Filipinos began firing.

The following day, General MacArthur issued his order to advance against the Filipino troops. No attempt was made to find out the cause of the shooting and to "see whether the former passive condition could be maintained."

The rift had widened into an armed conflict. The Filipino-American hostilities had begun.

*   *   *

It is difficult to believe that the Americans came to the Philippines merely to expel the Spaniards and so defeat them in a war of their own making. There was, in the first place, [General Wesley] Merritt's refusal to allow Aguinaldo and his men to participate in the conquest of Manila. The reason given, namely, that the Filipinos, if allowed to do so, might rape the Spanish women and kill their children and menfolk, had no justification in fact and served as a crude rationalization of his unjust act. No less than General Anderson, in his letter to the Adjutant General, dated December 24, 1898, testified that "they [the Filipinos] maintained good discipline." It is probable that Merritt, in pursuing a policy that was contrary to the interests of his ally, wanted to hog the limelight for himself, on the one hand, and, on the other, to consolidate his position militarily in preparation for an expected or possible conflict with the Filipinos. Whether he was acting on his own or whether he was officially instructed by Washington to act in the manner he did showed that there was from the very beginning an intention to take the Philippines or a part of it.

In the second place, the American Government, in sending a continuous stream of recruits to the Philippines, showed that it had no intention to help the Filipinos to their feet as it did to the Cubans. Since the American imperialists could not very well gobble up Cuba without arousing the moral ire of the world, particularly of Spain, Germany, and France, they had to get compensation elsewhere. The Philippines, then unknown even to the literate Americans, was some such compensation. Implying that the Filipinos were still savages, President McKinley declared it his policy "to civilize" the Filipinos. It was only when the imperialist groups had gotten the upper hand in the American political scene that McKinley frankly admitted American intention in the Philippines. His pious avowal that he walked up and down the corridor of the White House and fell to his knees to pray the Almighty to give him light was a fiction that he foisted on the gullible sector of the American public in order to make him appear as a sort of Sir Galahad in the purity of his aims.

Lastly, it may be recalled that once in possession of the City of Manila (Intramuros), the American military authorities in the Philippines refused to truckle to Aguinaldo in so far as political questions were concerned, but nevertheless recognized him as the legitimate Filipino leader when they wanted concessions from him. There was in this attitude an ambivalence that can be explained by a lack of moral compunction in the American military. Had the Americans been disposed to let the Filipinos carve out their destiny they would have left the Phillipines as soon as the surrender of Manila was consummated. That they did not but on the contrary assumed a hostile attitude toward Aguinaldo and his government proved that, once the Spaniards were conquered, they were ready to junk the Filipino allies and conquer them, if need be, to bring American goods safely to this side of the Pacific. Nobody but the extremely naive would believe the official American rationalization that McKinley and his host of advisers did not know at the outset what to do with the Philippines. The rationalization is now understood to be a piece of propaganda to calm down the fears of the American anti-imperialists and, especially, the bulk of the American public, whose national experience had been to look askance at any trace of imperialistic pretensions. If the final decision to take the Philippines was put off to a later date, it was not because McKinley and the men around him had no intention to subjugate the American ally, but because the American public had not been sufficiently prepared to accept the idea of American imperialism. Only when this seemed certain did McKinley and his propagandists—the military, the businessmen, and the Protestant missionaries —make known his final decision to the American peace Commissioners in Paris.

Such was the ruthlessness with which Aguinaldo and the Filipino Government were treated by the American authorities that even the American Consul in Manila, O. F. Williams, said in a dispatch to the State Department:

Aguinaldo was aided to return here—helped to rifles—permitted to take cannon from warships sunk by us—and cannon, ammunition and stores from an arsenal surrendered to our forces,—allowed to land arms from China,—given arms taken at Subig [sic],—entrusted with prisoners there taken, and so, by the world's fair understanding was and is our ally—a Congress even, to the contrary notwithstanding and under the law of Nations and by the common law of Agency we, the Principal become responsible for reimbursement and proper indemnification. This is law! It is right! And better than all it is policy and wise economy.

If as an ally or agent Aguinaldo and his forces be fairly dealt with our flag will be hailed forever here, and so meager has been his pay to soldiers, and so meager his war commissary that his total war expense, which I claim is our debt, is not one-tenth if indeed one-one-hundredth part of what it would have cost our forces to accomplish the same results for our good.

Obviously, Consul Williams had a conscience and openly admitted to his superior in the State Department that the American policy in the Philippines was unjust, particularly because the Filipinos, as allies of the Americans, deserved a better treatment than was shown to them. But the military, represented by Merritt and, later, by Otis, viewed Aguinaldo's government as a doormat to be trampled upon when the proper occasion arose. Nor were Merritt and Otis honest enough to acknowledge Aguinaldo's important role in restoring a semblance of order in places where there was near-anarchy. Said Williams:

Small garrisons of Spanish here and there have been captured by Aguinaldo—have been uniformly well treated—but this finally broke

Spanish power—we Americans did this only at Cavite and Manila.
Aguinaldo did the rest over nearly all this Insular Empire. It is like one
belligerent holding New York and Brooklyn with the rest of their
state and all New England beyond its reach and control.

We may laugh at the quasi government of Aguinaldo since May 1,
but his is the only government this great island, and others also,
have had—and but for him and his subordinates anarchy, riot and
murder would have terrorized several millions of people.

* * *

Remember that owing to unsettled conditions our Commanders did
not even pretend control beyond a narrow zone about Cavite and
Manila. Indeed, they openly declared they had none—hence as Spanish
power was broken, Aguinaldo prevented anarchy.

But Williams' was a lone voice in the wilderness. The military, contemptuously disdaining Aguinaldo and what he represented, stuck to their guns and thus prepared the way for the Filipino-American hostilities. Had Aguinaldo listened to his military advisers who believed that the Americans should be attacked while they were still numerically weak, perhaps the history of the Philippines would have taken a different course.

selected bibliography

The study of American imperialism and anti-imperialism at the turn of the century is an exciting scholarly field, and it has attracted a considerable number of authors. Their books and articles provide a wide array of interpretation and subject matter, and the curious student should follow his interest into some of the works mentioned below. This bibliography focuses on the most recent secondary literature; citations for older studies and primary sources, and a more extensive list of works, can be found in the bibliographies of the books listed below.

American imperialism in the late nineteenth century was part of an international trend. For this larger context and for comparisons with European imperialism, see Robin Winks, "Imperialism," in *The Comparative Approach to American History,* ed. C. Vann Woodward (New York, 1968), pp. 253–70; Robert Strausz-Hupé and Harry W. Hazard, eds., *The Idea of Colonialism* (New York, 1958); David K. Fieldhouse, *The Colonial Empires: A Comparative Survey* (London, 1966); George H. Nadel and Perry Curtis, eds., *Imperialism and Colonialism* (New York, 1964), a handy paperback book that demonstrates the complexity of interpretation and fact; Parker T. Moon, *Imperialism and World Politics* (New York, 1947), a dated but provocative book. A. P. Thornton, *Doctrines of Imperialism* (New York, 1965); Richard Koebner, *Empire* (Cambridge, England, 1961); and Richard Koebner and H. D. Schmidt, *Imperialism: The Story and Significance of a Political Word, 1840–1960* (Cambridge, England, 1963), discuss the several and changing meanings of and explanations for empire and imperialism. Well researched is William L. Langer's *The Diplomacy of Imperialism* (New York, 1965). Two collections of essays present the European historiographical controversy centering largely on the question of the Marxist or economic interpretation of imperialism: Robin W. Winks, ed., *British Imperialism: Gold, God, Glory* (New York, 1963), and Harrison M. Wright, ed., *The "New*

141

Imperialism": Analysis of Late Nineteenth-Century Expansion (Lexington, Mass., 1961). Both carry useful bibliographies on European imperialism.

General studies of the late nineteenth century, which weave domestic and foreign policies together, include Carlton J. H. Hayes, *A Generation of Materialism, 1871–1900* (New York, 1941), on Europe, and on the United States, John A. Garraty, *The New Commonwealth, 1877–1890* (New York, 1968); Ray Ginger, *Age of Excess* (New York, 1965); Harold U. Faulkner, *Politics, Reform and Expansion, 1890–1900* (New York, 1959); and Robert Wiebe, *The Search for Order, 1877–1920* (New York, 1967). For a unique study of America's self-image, see Paul C. Nagel, *This Sacred Trust: American Nationality, 1798–1898* (New York, 1971).

Scholars of differing persuasions have written general interpretive works on American foreign policy and expansionism. William A. Williams, *The Tragedy of American Diplomacy* (New York, 1962), finds American imperialism to be out of tune with American ideals and motivated by economic factors. George F. Kennan, in *American Diplomacy, 1900–1950* (Chicago, 1951), concludes that American foreign policy has lacked realism. Dexter Perkins, in *The American Approach to Foreign Policy* (New York, 1962), writes that "the United States has no reason to apologize for its record." Robert E. Osgood, *Ideals and Self-Interest in America's Foreign Relations* (Chicago, 1953), finds "popular impulses" rather than a calculation of power governing American diplomacy. Useful interpretive textbooks include Norman Graebner, ed., *Ideas and Diplomacy: Readings in the Intellectual Tradition of American Foreign Policy* (New York, 1962), and Wayne S. Cole, *An Interpretive History of American Foreign Relations* (Homewood, Ill., 1968).

For contrasting overviews of late nineteenth-century American diplomacy, consult Walter LaFeber, *The New Empire: An Interpretation of American Expansion, 1860–1898* (Ithaca, 1963); William A. Williams, *The Roots of the Modern American Empire* (New York, 1969); Ernest R. May, *Imperial Democracy: The Emergence of America as a Great Power* (New York, 1961); Foster R. Dulles, *Prelude to World Power* (New York, 1965); Thomas A. Bailey, "America's Emergence as a World Power: The Myth and the Verity," *Pacific Historical Review* 30 (February 1961): 1–16; John A. S. Grenville and George B. Young, *Politics, Strategy, and American Diplomacy: Studies in Foreign Policy, 1873–1917* (New Haven, 1967); Marilyn Blatt Young, "American Expansion 1870–1900: The Far East," in Barton J. Bernstein, ed., *Towards a New Past* (New York, 1968), pp. 176–201; Milton Plesur, *America's Outward Thrust: Approaches to Foreign Affairs, 1865–1890* (DeKalb, Ill., 1971); Paul S. Holbo, "Economics, Emotion, and Expansion: An Emerging Foreign Policy," in *The Gilded Age,* ed. H. Wayne Morgan (Syracuse, 1970), pp. 199–221; Paolo E. Coletta, ed., *Threshold to American Internationalism: Essays on the Foreign Relations of William McKinley* (New York, 1970); Robert Levin, "An Interpretation of American Imperialism," *Journal of Economic History* 32 (March 1972): 316–60.

Most historians now agree that the imperialism of the 1890s had a long preparatory period. Richard Van Alstyne, *The Rising American Empire* (New

York, 1960), stresses the continuity of American imperialism from colonial origins. Joining this work and some of the studies mentioned above in studying the era before the 1890s are Walter R. Herrick, Jr., *The American Naval Revolution* (Baton Rouge, La., 1966), and Harold and Margaret Sprout, *The Rise of American Naval Power: 1776–1918* (Princeton, N.J., 1939), which discuss improvement in the American navy. Two articles that analyze the intellectual roots of expansion are Julius W. Pratt, "The Ideology of American Expansion," in *Essays in Honor of William E. Dodd,* ed. Avery O. Craven (Chicago, 1935), pp. 335–53, and Charles Vevier, "American Continentalism: An Idea of Expansion, 1845–1910," *American Historical Review* 65 (January 1960): 323–35. Frederick Merk, *Manifest Destiny and Mission in American History* (New York, 1963), and Albert K. Weinberg, *Manifest Destiny* (Baltimore, Md., 1935), interpret American justifications for expansion. David M. Pletcher, *The Awkward Years: American Foreign Relations under Garfield and Arthur* (Columbia, Mo., 1962), covers the years 1881–85 in detail. Sylvia Masterman, *The Origins of International Rivalry in Samoa, 1845–1884* (Stanford, 1934), demonstrates early American interest in the Pacific.

There are a number of studies that deal specifically with America's involvement in Hawaii. See Merze Tate, *The United States and the Hawaiian Kingdom: A Political History* (New Haven, Conn., 1965), and *Hawaii: Reciprocity or Annexation* (East Lansing, Mich., 1968); Sylvester K. Stevens, *American Expansion in Hawaii, 1842–1898* (Harrisburg, Pa., 1945); William A. Russ, Jr., *The Hawaiian Republic 1894–1898, Its Struggle to Win Annexation* (Selinsgrove, Pa., 1961); R. S. Kuykendall, *The Hawaiian Kingdom, 1778–1893,* 3 vols. (Honolulu, 1938–67).

Other background works include a biography of a leading early imperialist: Glyndon G. Van Deusen, *William Henry Seward* (New York, 1967). Two episodes in British-American competition are discussed in W. D. McIntyre, "Anglo-American Rivalry in the Pacific: The British Annexation of the Fiji Islands in 1874," *Pacific Historical Review* 29 (November 1960): 361–80, and Walter LaFeber, "The Background of Cleveland's Venezuelan Policy: A Reinterpretation," *American Historical Review* 65 (July 1961): 947–67. Interesting is Kenneth M. MacKenzie, *The Robe and the Sword: The Methodist Church and the Rise of American Imperialism* (Washington, D.C., 1961). For the congressional-presidential confrontation over expansion see Jeanette P. Nichols, "The United States Congress and Imperialism, 1861–1897," *Journal of Economic History* 21 (December 1961): 526–38.

For the relationship between racism and imperialism, consult: Paul F. Boller, Jr., *American Thought in Transition: The Impact of Evolutionary Naturalism, 1865–1900* (Chicago, 1969); Richard Hofstadter, *Social Darwinism in American Thought* (Boston, 1955); James P. Shenton, "Imperialism and Racism," in *Essays in American Historiography,* eds. Donald Sheehan and Harold C. Syrett (New York, 1960), pp. 230–50; Philip W. Kennedy, "The Racial Overtones of Imperialism as a Campaign Issue, 1900," *Mid-America* 48 (July 1966): 196–205; Philip W. Kennedy, "Race and American Expansion in Cuba

and Puerto Rico, 1895–1905," *Journal of Black Studies* 1 (March 1971):
306–16; Rubin Francis Weston, *Racism in U.S. Imperialism* (Columbia, S.C.,
1972).

American economic expansion abroad after the Civil War is treated by the
works of LaFeber, Holbo, Williams, Plesur, and Young cited above. Also useful
are Benjamin H. Williams, *Economic Foreign Policy of the United States*
(New York, 1929); Mira Wilkins, *The Emergence of Multinational Enterprise:
American Business Abroad from the Colonial Era to 1914* (Cambridge, Mass.,
1970); Lloyd C. Gardner, ed., *A Different Frontier* (Chicago, 1966); Cleona
Lewis, *America's Stake in International Investment* (Washington, D.C., 1939);
William A. Williams, *The Contours of American History* (Cleveland, Ohio,
1961); Howard B. Schonberger, *Transportation to the Seaboard: A Study in the
"Communication Revolution" and American Foreign Policy, 1860–1900*
(Westport, Conn., 1971). For international finance, see Herbert Feis, *Europe
the World's Banker, 1870–1914* (New Haven, Conn., 1930). For case studies,
consult David M. Pletcher, *Rails, Mines, and Progress: Seven American
Promoters in Mexico, 1867–1911* (Ithaca, N.Y., 1958); Fred H. Harrington,
*God, Mammon, and the Japanese: Dr. Horace N. Allen and Korean-American
Relations, 1884–1905* (Madison, Wis., 1944); Robert B. Davies, " 'Peacefully
Working to Conquer the World': The Singer Manufacturing Company in
Foreign Markets, 1854–1889," *Business History Review* 43 (Autumn 1969):
299–325; Morton Rothstein, "America in the International Rivalry for the
British Wheat Market," *Mississippi Valley Historical Review* 47 (December
1960): 401–18; Thomas G. Paterson, "American Businessmen and Consular
Service Reform, 1890's to 1906," *Business History Review* 40 (Spring 1966):
77–97; Merle Curti, "America at the World Fairs, 1841–1893," *American
Historical Review* 55 (July 1950): 833–56.

There are numerous accounts of the coming of the Spanish-American War and
its conduct. Walter Millis, *The Martial Spirit* (Boston, 1931), is a popular
treatment. Julius W. Pratt, *Expansionists of 1898* (Baltimore, Md., 1938),
emphasizes ideological factors. Frank Friedel, *The Splendid Little War* (Boston,
1958), is packed with pictures and a colorful commentary. H. Wayne
Morgan, *America's Road to Empire* (New York, 1965), applauds American
diplomacy. For the role of the mass media and public opinion in the coming of
the war, see Marcus M. Wilkerson, *Public Opinion and the Spanish-American
War: A Study in War Propaganda* (Baton Rouge, La., 1932); Joseph E.
Wisan, *The Cuban Crisis as Reported in the New York Press, 1895–1898*
(New York, 1934); Charles H. Brown, *The Correspondent's War* (New
York, 1967). Paul S. Holbo stresses "emotions" in "The Convergence
of Moods and the Cuban-Bond 'Conspiracy of 1898,' " *Journal of American
History* 55 (June 1968): 54–72. The "psychic crisis" thesis is expounded
by Richard Hofstadter, *The Paranoid Style in American Politics* (New York,
1965). An economic interpretation is given by Philip S. Foner, "Why the
United States Went to War with Spain in 1898," *Science and Society* 32
(Winter 1968): 39–65. May's *Imperial Democracy* discusses the response of
European nations to American diplomacy before, during, and after the war.
David Healy, *U.S. Expansionism: The Imperialist Urge in the 1890s*

(Madison, Wis., 1970), surveys a number of leaders and ideas. Useful are
Graham A. Cosmas, *An Army for Empire: The United States Army in
the Spanish-American War* (Columbia, Mo., 1971), and William R. Braisted,
The United States Navy in the Pacific, 1898–1907 (Austin, Texas, 1958).
Ronald Spector, "Who Planned the Attack on Manila Bay?" *Mid-America* 53
(April 1971): 94–104, argues that the navy was more confused than Grenville
and Young believe in their *Politics, Strategy, and American Diplomacy.*

Questions of leadership are treated in Gerald G. Eggert, "Our Man in
Havana: Fitzhugh Lee," *Hispanic American Historical Review* 47 (November
1967): 463–85, which finds the American consul-general to be an
aggressive individual urging intervention, in part to promote private
speculation in Cuba; Paul S. Holbo, "Presidential Leadership in Foreign
Affairs: William McKinley and the Turpie-Foraker Amendment," *American
Historical Review* 72 (July 1967): 1321–35, a study of McKinley's success
in defeating a congressional resolution recognizing the Cuban revolutionary
government; and H. Wayne Morgan, ed., *Making Peace with Spain: The
Diary of Whitelaw Reid, September–December 1898* (Houston, Texas,
1968), about an American peace commissioner.

Leading imperialists are discussed in Margaret Leech, *In the Days of
McKinley* (New York, 1959); H. Wayne Morgan, *William McKinley and His
America* (Syracuse, N.Y., 1963); John Braeman, *Albert J. Beveridge:
American Nationalist* (Chicago, 1971); John Garraty, *Henry Cabot Lodge*
(New York, 1953); William A. Williams, "Brooks Adams and American
Expansion," *New England Quarterly* 25 (June 1952): 217–32. Theodore
Roosevelt has numerous biographers and studies devoted to his foreign
policy ideas. Some of the best include Howard K. Beale, *Theodore
Roosevelt and the Rise of America to World Power* (Baltimore, Md., 1956);
David H. Burton, *Theodore Roosevelt: Confident Imperialist* (Philadelphia,
Pa., 1969); William H. Harbaugh, *Power and Responsibility* (New York,
1961); John M. Blum, *The Republican Roosevelt* (Cambridge, Mass., 1954).
The secretaries of state can be surveyed in Samuel Flagg Bemis, ed., *The
American Secretaries of State and Their Diplomacy* (several volumes), which
offers flattering accounts.

Historians have given some attention to the relationship of socialists, labor
leaders, and blacks to the Spanish-American War and imperialism: Howard H.
Quint, "American Socialists and the Spanish-American War," *American
Quarterly* 10 (Summer 1958): 131–41; Jack A. Clarke, "Spanish Socialists
and the Spanish-American War," *Mid-America* 40 (October 1958): 229–31;
Delber L. McKee, "Samuel Gompers, the A.F. of L., and Imperialism,
1895–1900," *The Historian* 21 (February 1959): 187–99; Ronald Radosh,
"American Labor and the Anti-Imperialist Movement," *Science and Society*
28 (Winter 1964): 91–100; John C. Appel, "The Unionization of Florida
Cigarmakers and the Coming of the War with Spain," *Hispanic American
Historical Review* 36 (February 1956): 38–49; Perry E. Giankos, "The
Spanish-American War and the Double Paradox of the Negro American,"
Phylon 26 (Spring 1965): 34–50; Willard B. Gatewood, Jr., *"Smoked
Yankees" and the Struggle for Empire: Letters from Negro Soldiers,*

1898–1902 (Urbana, Ill., 1971); George P. Marks, ed., *The Black Press Views American Imperialism, 1898–1900* (New York, 1971).

Studies of anti-imperialism and the anti-imperialists include E. Berkeley Tompkins, *Anti-Imperialism in the United States: The Great Debate, 1890–1920* (Philadelphia, Pa., 1970); Robert L. Beisner, *Twelve Against Empire* (New York, 1968); Fred H. Harrington, "The Anti-Imperialist Movement in the United States," *Mississippi Valley Historical Review* 22 (September 1935): 211–30; John W. Rollins, "The Anti-Imperialists and Twentieth Century American Foreign Policy," *Studies on the Left* 3, no. 1 (1962): 9–24; Richard E. Welch, Jr., "Motives and Policy Objectives of Anti-Imperialists, 1898," *Mid-America* 51 (April 1969): 119–29; Maria C. Lanzar, "The Anti-Imperialist League," several long articles (essentially constituting a book) published over the period 1930–33 in *The Philippine Social Science Review*.

Christopher Lasch, "The Anti-Imperialists, the Philippines, and the Inequality of Man," *Journal of Southern History* 24 (August 1958): 319–31, labels them racists. The role of intellectuals and writers is treated in Fred H. Harrington, "Literary Aspects of American Anti-Imperialism," *New England Quarterly* 10 (December 1937): 650–67. Two essays present earlier anti-imperialist critiques of American foreign policy: Donald M. Dozer, "Anti-Expansionism during the Johnson Administration," *Pacific Historical Review* 12 (September 1943): 253–75, and Robert L. Beisner, "Thirty Years Before Manila: E. L. Godkin, Carl Schurz, and Anti-Imperialism in the Gilded Age," *The Historian* 30 (August 1968): 561–77. An interesting comparison is drawn in Robert L. Beisner, "1898 and 1968: The Anti-Imperialists and the Doves," *Political Science Quarterly* 85 (June 1970): 187–216. Dissenters from the War of 1812, the war with Mexico, and the Spanish-American War are superficially discussed in Samuel E. Morison, Frederick Merk, and Frank Freidel, *Dissent in Three American Wars* (Cambridge, Mass., 1970).

Anti-imperialist leaders, because many of them were prominent Americans, have interested scholars, most of whom are admirers. For William Jennings Bryan, see Merle E. Curti, *Bryan and World Peace* (Northhampton, Mass., 1931); Paul W. Glad, *The Trumpet Soundeth* (Lincoln, Nebr., 1960); and Paolo E. Coletta, *William Jennings Bryan,* 3 vols. (Lincoln, Nebr., 1964–69). For other anti-imperialists, consult Richard E. Welch, Jr., *George Frisbie Hoar and the Half-Breed Republicans* (Cambridge, Mass., 1971); Tilden G. Edelstein, *Strange Enthusiasm: A Life of Thomas Wentworth Higginson* (New Haven, Conn., 1968); William G. Whittaker, "Samuel Gompers: Anti-Imperialist," *Pacific Historical Review* 38 (November 1969): 429–45; Edward N. Burns, *David Starr Jordan* (Stanford, Calif., 1953); Claude N. Fuess, *Carl Schurz, Reformer* (New York, 1932); William Gibson, "Mark Twain and Howells: Anti-Imperialists," *New England Quarterly* 20 (December 1947): 435–70; Philip S. Foner, *Mark Twain: Social Critic* (New York, 1958); Louis J. Budd, *Mark Twain: Social Philosopher* (Bloomington, Ind., 1962); Maxwell Geismar, *Mark Twain: An American Prophet* (Boston, 1970); Edward C. Kirkland, *Charles Francis Adams, Jr., 1835–1915: The*

Patrician at Bay (Cambridge, Mass., 1965); John C. Farrell, *Beloved Lady: A History of Jane Addams' Ideas on Reform and Peace* (Baltimore, Md., 1967); William N. Armstrong, *E. L. Godkin and American Foreign Policy, 1865–1900* (New York, 1957); Joseph F. Wall, *Andrew Carnegie* (New York, 1970); David S. Patterson, "Andrew Carnegie's Quest for World Peace," *Proceedings of the American Philosophical Society* 114 (October 1970): 371–83.

Much work needs to be done on comparative anti-imperialist movements in England, which especially aroused dissenters because of the Boer War, and the United States. For British anti-imperialism, see Bernard Porter, *Critics of Empire: British Radical Attitudes to Colonialism in Africa, 1895–1914* (London, 1968); A. P. Thornton, *The Imperial Idea and Its Enemies* (London 1959); R. C. Brown, "Goldwin Smith and Anti-Imperialism," *Canadian Historical Review* 43 (June 1962): 93–105.

For American involvement in the Far East, the Open Door notes, and imperialism, see Thomas McCormick, *The China Market* (Chicago, 1967); Kwang-Ching Lui, *Americans and Chinese: A Historical Essay and a Bibliography* (Cambridge, Mass., 1963); Charles S. Campbell, *Special Business Interests and the Open Door Policy* (New Haven, Conn., 1951); A. Whitney Griswold, *The Far Eastern Policy of the United States* (New York, 1938); Marilyn Blatt Young, *The Rhetoric of Empire* (Cambridge, Mass., 1968); Paul A. Varg, *The Making of a Myth: The United States and China, 1897–1912* (East Lansing, Mich., 1968); Raymond A. Esthus, "The Changing Concept of the Open Door, 1899–1910," *Mississippi Valley Historical Review* 46 (December 1959): 435–54.

Toward the end of the century, British-American relations became more cordial, and the British were not unfriendly toward the American imperialist course in Latin America and the Far East. For works on the Anglo-American flirtation and its impact on imperialism, see Charles S. Campbell, *Anglo-American Understanding, 1898–1903* (Baltimore, Md., 1957); R. G. Neale, *Great Britain and United States Expansion: 1898–1900* (East Lansing, Mich., 1966); Bradford Perkins, *The Great Rapprochement: England and the United States, 1895–1914* (New York, 1968); Alexander E. Campbell, *Great Britain and the United States, 1895–1903* (London, 1960); John A. S. Grenville, *Lord Salisbury and Foreign Policy: The Close of the Nineteenth Century* (London, 1970).

To secure control of the Philippines, the United States had to quell an insurrection led by Emilio Aguinaldo. Death and destruction were widespread, and the American institutions imposed on the conquered Filipinos further disrupted Philippine life. Leon Wolff, *Little Brown Brother* (Garden City, N.Y., 1961), is frank in its condemnation of American action. Massacres are described in Stuart C. Miller, "Our Mylai of 1900: Americans in the Philippine Insurrection," *Transaction* 7 (September 1970): 19–28, and Rienara P. Weinert, "The Massacre at Balanziga," *American History Illustrated,* I (August 1966): 5–11, 37–40. The Senate hearings of 1902 on American brutality have been excerpted by Henry F. Graff, ed., *American Imperialism and the Philippine Insurrection* (Boston, 1969). For an important letter by a military colonel depicting American behavior, see Melvin G. Holli, "A View of the American Campaign Against 'Filipino Insurgents': 1900," *Philippine Studies* 17 (January 1969): 97–111. For William Howard Taft's appointment and investigation of the chaos in the Philippines, consult Ralph E. Minger, "From Law to Diplomacy: The Summons to the Philippines," *Mid-America* 53 (April 1971): 103–20. Important studies from the Filipino point of view are Teodoro A. Agoncillo, *Malolos: The Crisis of the Republic* (Quezon City, Philippines, 1960) and Teodoro A. Agoncillo and Oscar M. Alfonso, *History of the Filipino People* (Quezon City, Philippines, 1967). Agoncillo gives briefer coverage in *A Short History of the Philippines* (New York, 1969). Emilio Aguinaldo recalls his part in *A Second Look at America* (New York, 1957).

For the story of American colonialism in the Philippines after 1900, see Julius W. Pratt, *America's Colonial Experiment* (New York, 1950); Garel A. Grunder and William E. Livezey, *The Philippines and the United States* (Norman, Okla., 1951); Whitney T. Perkins, *Denial of Empire: The United States and Its Dependencies* (Leyden, 1962); Shirley Jenkins, *American Economic Policy Towards the Philippines* (Stanford, 1954); John A. Beadles, "The Debate in the United States Concerning Philippine Independence, 1912–1916," *Philippine Studies* 16 (July 1968): 421–41; Roy W. Curry, "Woodrow Wilson and Philippine Policy," *Mississippi Valley Historical Review* 41 (December 1954): 435–52; Thomas S. Hines, "The Imperial Facade: Daniel H. Burnham and American Architectural Planning in the Philippines," *Pacific Historical Review,* 41 (February 1972): 33–53; Frank T. Reuter, "American Catholics and the Establishment of the Philippine Public School System," *Catholic Historical Review* 49 (October 1963): 365–81; Bonifacio S. Salamanca, *The Filipino Reaction to American Rule, 1901–1913* (Hamden, Conn., 1968); Peter W. Stanley, "William Cameron Forbes: Proconsul in the Philippines [1904–1913]," *Pacific Historical Review* 35 (August 1966): 285–301; Theodore Friend, *Between Two Empires: The Ordeal of the Philippines, 1929–1946* (New Haven, Conn., 1965); Gerald E. Wheeler, "Republican Philippine Policy, 1921–1933," *Pacific Historical Review* 28 (November 1959): 377–90; Woodford Howard, "Frank Murphy and the Philippine Commonwealth," *Pacific Historical Review* 33 (February 1964): 45–68; several articles by Michael P. Onorato in *Philippine Studies* for 1965; Robert O. Tilman, "The Impact of American Education on the Philippines," *Asia,* no. 21 (Spring 1971): 66–80. For Guam, see Earl S. Pomeroy, *Pacific Outpost: American Strategy in Guam and Micronesia* (Stanford, Calif., 1951).

For American imperialism in Latin America after 1898, there are numerous works. Dana G. Munro, *Intervention and Dollar Diplomacy in the Caribbean, 1900–1921* (Princeton, N.J., 1964), denies that American business controlled American policy. Samuel F. Bemis, *The Latin American Policy of the United States* (New York, 1943), is a very traditional account reflecting the State Department's point of view. Also consult Richard W. Leopold, "The Emergence of America as a World Power: Some Second Thoughts," in *Change and Continuity in Twentieth-Century America,* eds. John Braeman et al.

(Columbus, Ohio, 1964), pp. 3–34. More critical are Robert F. Smith, *The United States and Cuba: Business and Diplomacy, 1917–1960* (New York, 1960); Kenneth F. Woods, " 'Imperialistic America': A Landmark in the Development of U.S. Policy Toward Latin America," *Inter-American Economic Affairs* 21 (Winter 1967): 55–72; David Green, *The Containment of Latin America* (Chicago, 1971).

The American domination of Cuba for many years after 1898 is well chronicled by historians. See, for example: David F. Healy, *The United States in Cuba, 1898–1902* (Madison, Wis., 1963); Alan R. Millett, *The Politics of Intervention: The Military Occupation of Cuba, 1906–1909* (Columbus, Ohio, 1968); Russel H. Fitzgibbon, *Cuba and the United States, 1900–1935* (Menaska, Wis., 1935); George Baker, "The Wilson Administration and Cuba, 1913–1921," *Mid-America* 46 (January 1964): 48–63; Carleton Beals, *The Crime of Cuba* (Philadelphia, Pa., 1934); James H. Hitchman, "The Platt Amendment Revisited: A Bibliographic Survey," *The Americas* 23 (April 1967): 343–69; T. P. Wright, Jr., "United States Electoral Intervention in Cuba," *Inter-American Economic Affairs* 13 (Winter 1959): 50–71; John M. Hunter, "Investment as a Factor in the Economic Development of Cuba, 1899–1935," *Inter-American Economic Affairs* 5 (Winter 1951): 82–100; Duvon C. Corbitt, "Cuban Revisionist Interpretation of Cuba's Struggle for Independence," *Hispanic American Historical Review* 43 (August 1963): 395–404; Hugh Thomas, *Cuba: The Pursuit of Freedom, 1762–1969* (New York, 1970). American activity in Puerto Rico shortly after its occupation is discussed in Edward J. Berbusse, *The United States in Puerto Rico, 1898–1900* (Chapel Hill, N.C., 1966).

This bibliography is selective. For listings of other studies and government documents, consult the bibliographies of the works cited above. Historians will continue to debate American imperialism and anti-imperialism. The conflicting interpretations that emerge seem to suggest uttter confusion. Yet the differing views produced by vigorous debate indicate a healthiness in historical inquiry. Readers of this collection are urged to join that debate by further reading and research.